# THE FIRST FIVE PS THAT CHANGED MY LIFE

## EMMANUEL ATOE

WESTBOW
PRESS®
A DIVISION OF THOMAS NELSON
& ZONDERVAN

WestBow Press books may be ordered through booksellers or by contacting:

WestBow Press
A Division of Thomas Nelson & Zondervan
1663 Liberty Drive
Bloomington, IN 47403
www.westbowpress.com
844-714-3454

ISBN: 978-1-6642-4259-3 (sc)
ISBN: 978-1-6642-4260-9 (e)

Print information available on the last page.

WestBow Press rev. date: 10/15/2021

# Contents

# The First Five P's That Changed My Life

"The first five Ps that Changed My Life" hopefully will change your life for good and for the best. Can five Letters really change the life of an individual? Can five alphabetic letters be so powerful to impact positive changes in a person's life? How can five letters impact your life to achieve what you would like to accomplish in life? Can it work for anyone? Can I apply them to my life? Will it work for me, or it is just a hose, i.e., fake? How can these five letters be useful to my life? How can I apply them to change my life for good? How will these five letters help me to accomplish my dreams and vision and aspiration.? Living your best life in five Ps is possible. Dr. Emmanuel O. Atoe wrote this life experiences book that is so powerful that it will change your story for good. If the principles explained in this book is applied correctly, you will achieve the desire of your heart.

## The Breath-Taking London City

If anyone had told me that five simple words could have so much impact in my life, I would have thought it was one of those fairy tales in the old children's book. The good news is that it is true, and I am glad to tell you the story trusting it will change your story for the best. "The Five Ps That Changed My Life" will change your life for good. It all started in an area not too distance from the one of the world's busiest railway station - Waterloo London in England. This busy station remains one of the largest stations in terms of floor space. I was a university student in London, United Kingdom.

I still believe that London is one of the most breathtakingly, beautiful, and exciting places in the world to live, especially for students, it is simply one of the best cities in the world to enjoy your college life and get your degree or college education. Although I later moved to another borough, but it all started in this area. I was at Lambeth borough which forms part of inner London known as south London. A former university student friend said it was named after "landing place for lambs." I don't really care much about the lamb thing, but all I know is that I very much enjoy the area the other side of the Thames lies an area filled with lots of great excitement and captivating sights, which is popularly known as the centre of London, that is the splendid and captivating City of Westminster.

Most young adults that travel to London to study or holidays must agree that they admire the distinct buildings. London is unique and its vibe is absolutely captivating, with the blending of the frenetic and extremely rushed hours and fast-paced live style coupled with the cold wind, and often drizzling but has the form of calmness and coolness, that can be felt in that early morning breeze that is so attractive and seductive to any individual that loves big city. Success they say is just cream on the cake, in this situation like it or not the "drizzling is the cream of this enthralling city".

One of the greatest ability God has given mankind is the wonderful gift of learning. How beautiful it is to go through this beautiful city to discover and learn about the various culture and beauty embedded in one of the most beautiful European cites. London is green with gardens, and some of the most fascinating Parks. How about the awesome garden for relaxing moments? I also love the good times in London's restaurants, one of the few places in the world where you can eat or buy almost everything you could possibly desire, from local fish and chips to Italian, you name it. Although I do not drink alcohol, so the Fridays and Saturday's nights or any other visits for that matter was not my "cup of tea", excuse my French, I meant to say, night outing drinking alcohol was not and still not my lifestyle, but I must admit that London is also known for its pubs.

The people who love live music like me, will admit that they can enjoy it and for student's free music time-out in the evening is life. Though it does not come cheap, expensive London's West End has world-renowned, theatres known world-wide for its great productions. It was a joy to see the musicals live. As a student, some of the world-class museums was learning with pleasure. Another good news and good thing as student were that sometimes, some of them were free, and believe it or not this was a source of blessing to us students. Some Saturdays, some of us visited the food markets for some of gastronomic delights.

Living in London is great but economically as a student it could be tough, challenging and a struggle financially wise, but you do not have to be despair. To be successful in this city or anywhere you are living, you must have a mind set with goals, never lose focus and be self-disciple. The initial goal was simply to complete my studies, have my degree and become IT banking and Telco Manager. However, as a student the pressing issue that needed urgent attention was to manage myself, my studies, and my finance properly. The question was if as a student you cannot learn to manage properly your finances, how can you learn to manage projects in the bank? That was the first question as a student that urgently needs an answer and I had to address properly.

The key to the next level was to solve this problem, deal properly with all the pressing issues involved and make sure that things work out properly and successfully, in other to achieve the desired goals. The rate of student dropping out from college after the first two years was not encouraging, alarming to be precise and the decision was to take my eyes off the negatives and focus on the positive. Sometimes it easier said than done. Do you notice that a lot of people tells you the first year at the university what they are going to do, and you really think they are going to take the world by storm, some speak about what they are going to do and achieve, only to see them after the first two semester in confusion and depression. Take a look at their faces and you do not need to ask them "how is the going?" because the weariness in their eyes shows they have lost the spark; the fire is gone, and they are already running on the reserve tanks. Why may you ask?

Why do people start with such fire, only to get very weary after the bell rang to start running instead of marching? Why do people crawl instead of walking or running when they had the intention at kick-off to run the race well and finish well? It is amazing how many gallons of energy was used for the kick-off, only to start weaving after some yards. Why you may ask, and you are not the only one because that is the question of humanity. As the saying goes it easier said than done, but you have to do something and fast, your words are particularly important but "action speaks louder than words" because time waits for no body and that includes you and me.

## The Power of Visualization or Imagination

The Lord reminded me of the story in the book of Genesis chapter 11 verse 3 to 9 (NIV), about "The Tower of Babel" At one time all the people of the world spoke the same language and used the same words. As the people migrated to the east, they found a plain in the land of Babylonia and settled there. *"They said to each other, "Come, let's make bricks and bake them thoroughly." They used brick instead of stone, and tar for mortar. Then they said, "Come, let us build ourselves a city, with a tower that reaches to the heavens, so that we may make a name for ourselves; otherwise, we will be scattered over the face of the whole earth. But the LORD came down to see the city and the tower the people were building. The LORD said, "If as one people speaking the same language, they have begun to do this, then nothing they plan to do will be impossible for them. Come, let us go down and confuse their language so they will not understand each other. So, the LORD scattered them from there over all the earth, and they stopped building the city. That is why it was called Babel because there the LORD confused the language of the whole world. From there the LORD scattered them over the face of the whole earth."*

In that way, the Lord scattered them all over the world, and they stopped building the city. That is why the city was called Babel, because that is where the Lord confused the people with different languages. In this way he scattered them all over the world. What a powerful story.

Let me draw your attention to this part of the story "After this, nothing these individuals set out to do or imagined [*to do*] or visualized [*to do*] will be impossible for them," That is called the power of visualization or imagination, a secret known and practice by most successful individuals. A well-known fact is that remarkably successful or influential individuals, practiced a revealed hidden secret or truth that enabled every one of them to achieve and live the good future they dreamt about. The question is what is it? Can everyone practice it? The truth is it not the exclusive property of few privilege individuals. As a matter of fact, some individuals do not read historical facts or learn from history or the success stories of men and women all over the world. The stories of successful men and women in various fields of life show a common factor irrespective of age, race, background, or origin.

Many of these individuals were good dreamers, who dreamt, (hopefully believing) of being what they finally achieved. They are living their good dreams. Most of us have seen or heard news interviews of sport men and women saying things like "I've dreamt about it from when I was little kids, lying in bed dreaming about it, getting that gold medal put around my necks on the podium or winning this trophy or scoring the winning goal or point, etc…." Most successful athletes, sportsmen and women, artist and entrepreneur saw themselves and practice behind the scenes what they are doing successful in the public. They all saw themselves living or achieving in their inner eye or mind what they accomplish in the natural. The same factor works unfortunately on the negative, about those who feed on back dreams, without hope and motivation for a good future. The good dreamers are highly motivated to live and knew what they wanted to do with their lives, even at the early stage of life (such a young age), while some individuals at a certain stage in their life (matured adults), eventually when they finally grasp this powerful truth and fact, and they start applying it to their situation.

The scripture says, in Psalm chapter 119 verse 15 (ESV) *"I will meditate on your precepts and fix my eyes on your ways."* God taught successful men in the bible a secret that most successful individual practices today, that has made them to successfully live their good dreams. It was not invented by man but by the living almighty wisdom of God. What is this secret we are talking about? It is simple but powerful, the art of visualizing their future. Visualization is not daydreaming or being idle. It is simply seeing the invisible, or you could say seeing your future with the eye of faith. It does not matter what other people think, say, or imagine about you but it is your own ability to see what nobody notices or imagined about you and your future. You must be able to imagine it and see a bright or brilliant achievement concerning your future in your mind's eye. This is not mind game most individual see themselves successful before they achieve success in real life.

## Confirmation by the testimony of two or three witnesses

Did God teach successful men in the bible a secret that most successful individual practices today, that has made them to successfully live their good dreams? The answer is absolutely, yes God did. The facts of every case must be established by the testimony of two or three witnesses, that is every fact is to be confirmed by the testimony of two or three witness. Paul is reiterating that while he "knows" there is sin in the church, even as an Apostle of Jesus, he will not cast a man out on hearsay: it must be confirmed in the proper process. The scripture says, in Deuteronomy chapter 19 verse 15 (NIV) "One witness is not enough to convict anyone accused of any crime or offense they may have committed. A matter must be established by the testimony of two or three witnesses." Every fact is to be confirmed by the testimony of two or three witnesses.

Most successful men and women start out acting what they are doing in real life. They use their imagination to create an ideal future for themselves. I am in no doubt suggesting daydreaming, folding their arms, sleeping and being idler or doing absolutely nothing. A little sleep, a little slumber, a little folding of the hands to rest, and poverty will come upon you like a robber, and want like an armed man. This is not about an individual that is without ambition, idle, lack initiative, showing no ambition and complacent individual. The book of Joshua chapter 1 verse 8 and 9 (NIV), says "Keep this Book of the Law always on your lips; meditate on it day and night, so that you may be careful to do everything written in it. Then you will be prosperous and successful. Have I not commanded you? Be strong and courageous. Do not be afraid; do not be discouraged, for the LORD your God will be with you wherever you go."

## The Power of Meditation and Visualization

Joshua chapter 1 verse 8 (NIV), says "Keep this Book of the Law always on your lips; meditate on it day and night, so that you may be careful to do everything written in it. Then you will be prosperous and successful." The word tells us to behold or to perceive through sight the word of God. Do not let the word depart from your eyes, keep it properly in your heart. Why? Because, what you behold, you become. So, you need to see images of what your life can look like. You must discipline yourself to stop looking at reality and start thinking positively, focusing on your goals. The truth of the matter is, you must see something with your "inner eyes" before you can physically have it. So, make your own dream video, vision, or hang pictures up of your expected good financial future, your ideal physical body, your dream vacation, your debt paid in full property, your marriage restored, your kids serving God and your business flourishing, etc…. Then with faith, patience and discipline make your daily, weekly, monthly, yearly success plan.

Most successful individuals always take further practical steps to further and surround themselves, to make visuals their dream. They put into action, by speaking it, acting it out continuously, they practice by faith as if it would one day be their future, athletics, showbiz, entrepreneur, inventor, you name it, whatever field of achievement, they eventually became what they visualized, imagined, or believed in their heart. These principles are not mind power or mind control or positive thinking invented by mankind, but they are biblical principles given by God to man in His Word to achieve success.

God told Abraham in Genesis chapter 13 verse 15 (NLT), "I am giving all this land, as far as you can see, to you and your descendants as a permanent possession." Until you see it, you are not entitled to it. That instruction simply indicates that without revelation there is no restoration. You have got to see it to have it. The story of Abram, who at 75 years old when God told him to move from his country of origin. Abraham obeyed and departed for a land that God would later reveal to him. He has faith in the Word of God and trusting God to lead him without a map, compass, or navigator, although he did not know where he was moving and the house he will live. In fact, everything was unknown to him regarding his destination, and it is seeming impossible. Abraham had to listen properly to the directions he received from God and his success depended on how well he listens to God directions and most especially obey them. He was led to the land of Canaan where he received the promise from God.

Genesis chapter 13 verse 14 to 17 (ESV) *"The LORD said to Abram, after Lot had separated from him, "Lift up your eyes and look from the place where you are, northward and southward and eastward and westward, for all the land that you see I will give to you and to your offspring forever. I will make your offspring as the dust of the earth, so that if one can count the dust of the earth, your offspring also can be counted. Arise, walk through the length and the breadth of the land, for I will give it to you."*

*"Lift-up your eyes and look from the place where you are …."* Abraham was told to lift-up his eyes several times and look. He made the decision to look up and see the promises of God, and whenever he changed what he was looking at, he changed his circumstance or situations. We can look at our circumstances, we can focus on our difficulties and hard circumstances, or we can lift-up our eyes and look beyond to the greatness God has in store for us. If you do not like where you are today, take a step of faith. Lift-up your eyes, look up, and take hold of the promises God has in store for your future. For some individuals it could be easy to get out of the comfortable zone, but God wants to stretch you, grow, and experience new things of greater success and influence.

Another moment in Abraham's life journey, immediately after Lot had gone, the Lord said to Abram, Genesis 13:14-17 (NLT) *"After Lot had gone, the LORD said to Abram, "Look as far as you can see in every direction - north and south, east, and west. I am giving all this land, as far as you can see, to you and your descendants as a permanent possession. And I will give you so many descendants that, like the dust of the earth, they cannot be counted! Go and walk through the land in every direction, for I am giving it to you."*

God also assured Abram more than once at the age of over 75 years old, when he had no child, that his children would be so numerous as to be uncountable. This situation that seems impossible to the natural eyes of mankind, led God to give him something to visualize, images, pictures or as the scripture says "vision", The scripture says in Genesis chapter 13 verse 16 (NIV) "I will make your offspring like the dust of the earth, so that if anyone could count the dust, then your offspring could be counted." God directed him to look at the dust and count, which, obviously he could not count.

The scripture says, in Genesis chapter 15 verse 5 (NIV) He took him outside and said, "Look up at the sky and count the stars, if indeed you can count them." Then he said to him, "So shall your offspring be." The word of The Lord came to Abraham in a vision, reassuring Abraham of God's protection and reward. Abraham responded with heartfelt concern, pointing out that the Promise maker still had not given him the desire of his heart, children. God assured Abraham once again that his heir would be his own flesh and blood, i.e., biological, or natural child, not a servant. God then showed Abraham in a vision star. God directed him to look-up and count the stars above, obviously he could not count all the above stars. Seeing it happen before it actual occurred, with visualization or picture, creates a burning hunger or desire with intense and sharp images, negative pictures, or blueprints necessary for the hope or faith to create or bring to pass that desired result. If an individual wants to achieve his [or her] dreams, that is certainly one of the most important requirements.

The scripture says Jeremiah chapter 1 verses 11 and 12 (NIV) says the word of the Lord came to me: "What do you see, Jeremiah?" "I see the branch of an almond tree," I replied. The Lord said to me, "You have seen correctly, for I am watching to see that my word is fulfilled." What do you see James, Janet, you can add your name to the list?" Visualization, blueprints, or mind picture is seeing with the eye of faith. The important fact is seeing yourself or imagined doing the exceptionally good thing you dream about or desire to achieve in the future. The advantage is to surround our environment with faith materials to assist our desired vision. We must learn to use our imagining positively to visualize our good future, the thing we desire to accomplish.

## Vision Tablet

Habakkuk 2 chapter 2 verses 2 to 3 (ESV) *"And the LORD answered me: "Write the vision; make it plain on tablets, so he may run who reads it. For still the vision awaits its appointed time; it hastens to the end - it will not lie. If it seems slow, wait for it; it will surely come; it will not delay."*

The almighty God instructed prophet Habakkuk, in Habakkuk chapter 2 verse 2 to 3 (ESV), to do exactly what the word of God is instructing t you and I to do today, "And the LORD answered me: Write the vision; make it plain on tablets, so he may run who reads it. For still the vision awaits its appointed time; it hastens to the end - it will not lie. If it seems slow, wait for it; it will surely come; it will not delay." It is not good to see nothing and seeing bad things or always imaging evil forces of darkness, difficulties, problems, etc. I am no doubt suggesting they do not exist. They exist but we know that greater is God that is us that the forces of darkness that are against us. In Christ we are more than conquerors. What is God asking you today? What do you see?

You have got to see something before you can have something. Individuals must learn to get the image of what they want and not what they do not want, although must people have the wrong picture continuously, change the image and switch on a good vision for your tomorrow. Take off that image you do not want everybody to see about your future. An individual who does not have time practicing visualization, is probably not interested deeply for success, those who practice it will confirm that everything they visualized did eventually happened. I really believe that one of the greatest joys in life is to accomplish in real life what you have visualized for years. The particularly good thing about it, is that what you visualized and put on your vision tablet will happen at the appointed time.

However, always have in mind that it is your vision, so do not go about sharing it with everyone immediately, because others may not understand it or share it. They may discourage you and hinder your focus. This vision is like the words of a book [scroll] that is closed and sealed. You may give the book to someone who can read and tell that person to read it. Your vision is a closed book to others, because it is personal and sealed in your heart. Do not expect others to be excited about your vision and share your passion, because they cannot read your vision book or tablet. Whatever others think or do not think about the vision will not prevent the vision from coming to pass at the appointed moment and time. "For I know the plans I have for you,' declares the LORD, 'plans to prosper you and not to harm you, plans to give you hope and a future." Jeremiah chapter 29 verse 11 (NIVUK)

## Declare your Future and Guard your Heart!

The scripture says, in 1 Peter chapter 3 verses 10 and 11 (NIV), For, "Whoever would love life and see good days must keep their tongue from evil and their lips from deceitful speech. They must turn from evil and do good; they must seek peace and pursue it." However, to do this you must first and foremost watch what you allow into your heart. It means. You must guard your heart attentively. Most successful men and women live their good dreams, that is living the good life they imagined for many years. You must learn to visualize achieving your goals no matter how difficult or what changes that confronts you in your journey of life. This will help you to focus on the goals you have set for yourself and making sure you are applying them in your life. This is your picture for future success, so let go off your mind eye, pictures of failure and pictures of past successes.

The scripture says, in Proverb chapter 4 verse 23 (NIV) "Above all else, guard your heart, for everything you do flows from it." That means that your heart is extremely valuable, your heart is under constant attack and your heart is the source of everything you do. "Above everything." He does not say, "If you get around to it" or "It would be nice if." No, he says, make it your top priority.

This is the real deal; you visualize your ideal future. The question is what do you see? Your present problems and difficulties? Behind payment in mortgage and lots of debt? Marital problems? Problems with children? Mails of unpaid Bills? Job loose or career problem? In the valley of Unfulfilled desires? Hopeless situation and circumstances? Inability to be fulfilled in life.?

It is time to get out from the valley. The scripture says in Ezekiel chapter 37 verses 1 to 14 (NIV). The story of the Valley of Dry Bones. The hand of the LORD was on me, and he brought me out by the Spirit of the LORD and set me in the middle of a valley; it was full of bones. He led me back and forth among them, and I saw a great many bones on the floor of the valley, bones that were very dry. He asked me, "Son of man, can these bones live? I said, Sovereign LORD, you alone know." Then he said to me, Prophesy to these bones and say to them, 'Dry bones, hear the word of the LORD! This is what the Sovereign LORD says to these bones: I will make breath enter you, and you will come to life. I will attach tendons to you and make flesh come upon you and cover you with skin; I will put breath in you, and you will come to life. Then you will know that I am the LORD. So, I prophesied as I was commanded. And as I was prophesying, there was a noise, a rattling sound, and the bones came together, bone to bone. I looked, and tendons and flesh appeared on them, and skin covered them, but there was no breath in them. Then he said to me, Prophesy to the breath; prophesy, son of man, and say to it, this is what the Sovereign LORD says: Come, breath, from the four winds and breathe into these slain, that they may live. So, I prophesied as he commanded me, and breath entered them; they came to life and stood up on their feet - a vast army. Then he said to me: Son of man, these bones are the people of Israel. They say our bones are dried up and our hope is gone; we are cut off. Therefore, prophesy and say to them: This is what the Sovereign LORD says: My people, I am going to open your graves and bring you up from them; I will bring you back to the land of Israel. Then you, my people, will know that I am the LORD, when I open your graves and bring you up from them. I will put my Spirit in you, and you will live, and I will settle you in your own land. Then you will know that I the LORD have spoken, and I have done it, declares the LORD." The Word of the almighty God tells us this powerful principle that what we see is not permanent but temporary, however on the other hand an individual will eventually become what look at constantly and continuously. We need to have the good images or pictures God puts inside of us.

We need to visualize better pictures or images about the direction we want your life to go. The scripture says, in Psalms chapter 1 verse 1 through 3 (NASB1995), "How blessed is the man who does not walk in the counsel of the wicked, nor stand in the path of sinners, nor sit in the seat of scoffers! But his delight is in the law of the Lord, And in His law, he meditates day and night. He will be like a tree firmly planted by streams of water, which yields its fruit in its season. And its leaf does not wither; And in whatever he does, he prospers. You will become what you constantly put before your eyes. What you believe about yourself, and your future is certainly what you will eventually become. What you constantly put before your eyes may determine the outcome of your future. It could act as a compass to direct your choices and goals and your action consciously or unconsciously.

That is why taking a conscious step to visualize and act as if you already have accomplished your goals and dreams is so important. Successful individuals have various ways to visualize or picture what they would like to accomplish in a specific and precise manner, which could be within a short term, middle term, and long-term period, which could be a defined period from one year to over the next ten years and more. The scripture says in Philippians chapter 4 verse 8 (NIV) "Finally, brothers and sisters, whatever is true, whatever is noble, whatever is right, whatever is pure, whatever is lovely, whatever is admirable - if anything is excellent or praiseworthy - think about such things." I think were some of us missed it is that we are looking at our circumstances and my head, and our mind or limited knowledge is telling us we cannot make it because the obstacle is too high and the problem or mountain of debts, difficulties etc... cannot move away.

## Learn to Focus on the Good Things we Desire and Speak!

The good news is that we can turn your attention inward in your spirit, and change the picture, visualize the good things you-re expecting or desire because when you do this, your spirit will go to work to make this a reality. The scripture says, in Romans chapter 4 verse 17 (NIV) As it is written: "I have made you a father of many nations." He is our father in the sight of God, in whom he believed - the God who gives life to the dead and calls into being things that were not." The question is how you can exercise or release your faith? How do you express what you believe? Simple, through the words of your mouth. The bible says let the weak say they are strong. So, you confess or say what you desire not what you have which you do not desire. Everyone must learn the language of successful people.

You must be filled with God inside minded, believing in the ability the creator has placed in you to be an overcomer. This is the victory that overcomes the world our faith. Since we believe we speak the word of faith that we believe. The question is what is all this about? Individuals who are successful do not talk about their problems continuously, they know that no condition is permanent, and the situation is temporary if they insist for a change, by speaking the end result from the beginning instead of the present problem. The scripture says, in Mark chapter 11 verse 23 (NIV) "Truly I tell you, if anyone says to this mountain, 'Go, throw yourself into the sea,' and does not doubt in their heart but believes that what they say will happen, it will be done for them."

We must learn to focus on the things we desire or want and not waste our energy and time to the things we do not desire or want. Then visualize things un our heart to start to shift. We must not only believe we want a good life but believe we can have, and we do have a good life, because whatever is good in your heart will eventually come out in your mouth. Unfortunately, the words of most individuals do not reflect exactly the negative in their heart. If words have power, that means everything you say is shaping your life. You may not feel it or see it the minute you speak it, but those words are planting seeds. Just look back on your life or even where you are now. Do you remember speaking certain things about what you want or do not want to happen and now you are living it? Because words have power, we clearly must be intentional with what we speak. There could be times in your walk with God when you do feel inadequate, weak, tired, not capable of doing certain things or accomplishing certain goals. These are moment which can affect everyone, furthermore these are moments when you can change the whole direction of your life by speaking the Word of God, Life changing truth into your situation and over your life.

In times of trouble and times of doubt, remember the scripture in Philippians chapter 4 verse 13 (NIV) says "I can do all things through Christ who gives me strength." to find hope, comfort, strength most, especially perspective. God's words are filled with infinite promises of power, provision, strength, courage, hope, comfort, and encouragement. The scripture says, in Romans chapter 4 verse 17 (NIV) says, As it is written: "I have made you a father of many nations." He is our father in the sight of God, in whom he believed--the God who gives life to the dead and calls into being things that were not. Visualizing and speaking God's Life changing words over our life will change our circumstances for good. Joel chapter 3 verse 10 (NKJV) "Beat your plowshares into swords. And your pruning hooks into spears; Let the weak say, 'I am strong." The scripture does not say, "Let the weak say, "I am weak." But it says, "Let the weak say, "I am strong." The scripture is not telling us to live in denial about how we feel or to dwell in defeat, but it is telling us that there is better way to live, it is telling us to, by faith believe in God's word, which is the "Way" "Truth" and "Life" and to speak to your soul, God's Life changing words which will build you up and strengthen you in God to be victorious in life. The deal is this, start declaring where you want your life to go. Declare things. That you desire, for example I am enjoying a debt-free life, I am healthy, prospering, and successful, my business is doing great and not borrowing. I am successful in everything I put my hands to do. I can do all things through Christ who strengthens me. God is my source.

## The Right Mind-Set

I knew if I wanted to achieve my plans and purpose and to be successful in life, I must start from my mind. The amazing power of the word of God is that the moment your mindset changes, you change, it becomes easier to obey when you are persuaded, the light comes in and expels darkness, the eye of your understanding is opened because you are able to see what God sees in you and you are able to receive God's truths. "The entrance of Your words gives light; It gives understanding to the simple." Psalm 119:130 (NKJV) The entrance of word of God gives light that floods the mind with crystal clear instruction, that brings illumination when the words of God enter the heart without doubt, false humility, and unbelief. Then the word finds entrance into the mind and receives prompt attention which results in divine illumination.

The knowledge and understanding that comes from the word of truth that is revealed is so powerful that it completely dispels the darkness in the mind. There is such a Divine power in the revelation of the truth and the light of God's word, that very mental eye by which the light is received sends out powerful rays of inspiration that empowers us to communicate Devine truth or wisdom. This is a new day, to us which the Lord had made, to make us full of light and hope because as the blindfold begins to fall off accompanied by the destruction of the various fortresses that prevent us from receiving the Word and all the blessings of God. The wrong persuasions we had about ourselves, situation or circumstances, our family our future, including all those walls began to fall in the mind because the wisdom of God brings faith or believing the truth that the blessings of the Lord are accessible and attainable to us, who trust in God.

Do not be conformed to this world, but be transformed by the renewing of your mind, that you may prove what is the good and acceptable and perfect will of God. That is the mind-set of a good receiver and whatever mindset we have adopted consciously or subconsciously that has stopped God's blessings must come down or be destroyed like Jericho walls in our mind through the truth of the wisdom of God. Looking unto Jesus the author and finisher of our faith, our eyes will be open, and we will not be blind to the strategies or deceits of the enemy, in our life, family, business or work, finances, but adopting a mindset that is able change the way we think which eventually changes our persuasions. When our persuasion changes our behaviour. Some people try to change their behaviour without changing their belief system. This is not possible, we should never worry about changing our behaviour, because if we change what we believe, we can change our inappropriate behaviour.

I was crystal clear about this fact at the university that my limitation was in my mind... The mind-set is immensely powerful and particularly important factor that cannot be neglected, so I would encourage you to have the right mind-set. Let your mind be set or fixed that you are going to get the best out of this book and most especially you will successfully accomplish your life desire or good dreams. The story about the individuals who wanted to build the tower of babel tells us that the God almighty said "After this, nothing they "SET OUT TO DO" will be impossible for them! Genesis chapter 11 verse 6 (NLT), Another version (KJV) says it this way "now nothing will be restrained from them, which they "HAVE IMAGINED" to do. The third version (NIV) I have chosen to illustrate this truth to you is this "then nothing they "PLAN TO DO" will be impossible for them." What is my point? The point is that you like it or not your mind is always set on something at any time, day, or night. The question is what is your mind-set? What is in your mind, now?

Every child of God has the mind of Christ. Therefore, you have the mind to achieve God's plan and purpose for your life. You must have the fire to succeed burning in you that you cannot let anything stop you from doing what God has empowered you by His grace to do. Your present situation may make the dream seems impossible, a mountain insurmountable, thing may seem difficult to attain, impossible to accomplish, but you must guard your heart attentively, because out of your heart flows the issues of life. Therefore, preparing your minds for action, and being sober-minded, set your hope fully on the grace that will be brought to you at the revelation of Jesus Christ. If you are defeated in your mind, you may fail, the battle is in what you believe in your heart and what you are declaring daily to yourself that nobody knowns but only you in your mind.

Some people are so afraid to cast their net on the other side that they only pray for those little things that they believe are possible, forgetting that with God all things are possible, and all things are possible to those who believe. The challenge is in the mind. If you are defeated in your mind, you may be defeated in life. Be strong in the Lord and in the power of His might. It did not say be strong in yourself or the power of your might, as a matter of facts, the scripture says let the weak say I am strong. I believe that whatever God is telling you to do is going to see impossible. There is nobody in the bible and anyone that have a God given good dream that does not look too difficult and impossible to achieve. All good ideas, dreams, vision, and goals that an individual write in their plan book or vision book, may seem like fairy-tale or a mountain too high to climb. It may an impossible obstacle looking at your present situation and circumstances. The answer is with God all things are possible, so visualize the future not your present.

Have your mind set on the good picture of your future trusting God. The good news is your mind will always move toward the dominating images you keep before your eyes. The more you look at these pictures of your desire future, the more you desire them. Whatever is true, whatever is honourable, whatever is just, whatever is pure, whatever is lovely, whatever is commendable, if there is any excellence, if there is anything worthy of praise, think about these things. Virtue is not something innately ingrained when we are born, but rather, something we practice and improve on. Growing in virtue means forming a new habit and continuing that habit over time. The more you desire them, the more persistent you become in fulfilling them. Your spirit has a supernatural ability to connect to the Devine socket and figure out ways of achieving what you desire or your constant thoughts. Hope in the heart and positive expectation of the future God desire for you brings joy and peace into the heart of an individual and a happy family life. The family unites to improve for each other, and this is what leads to happier and healthier lives.

Cultivating this attitude helps us to develop confidence and a more meaningful life. It makes daily life much more pleasant because every day God loads us with blessings. Blessed be the Lord, who daily loaded us with benefits, even the God of our Salvation. The Scripture emphasizes that God daily loads us with benefits. The word 'loads' here depicts heaping in excess. Everyday God is supplying us His blessings in excess, more than we can handle. God just does not give us to survive, but He supplies us in excess, abundantly because that is God's way of doing things. That is why Jesus came that we might have life and might have [it] abundantly.

# *Prayer*

Prayer and meditation are the birthplace of a successful life. There is nothing like having a clear vision, goals, strong focus, concentration on purpose and having a plan to do one thing at a time without vain thoughts. In John chapter 14 verse 13 (NIV), "And I will do whatever you ask in my name, so that the Father may be glorified in the Son." Everyone that ask shall be given because your Father in heaven give good gifts to those who ask him! This gives confident in praying. My anchor verse in prayer was in Matthew 7 verse 7 and 8 (NIV), which says "Ask and it will be given to you; seek and you will find; knock and the door will be opened to you. For everyone who asks receives; the one who seeks finds; and to the one who knocks, the door will be opened." We must dedicate time each day for prayer, meditation, or mindfulness to helps us connect with the plan and purpose of God.

The power to connect with God helps us to have hope, especially in difficult moments. Prayer and meditation are the first step for anyone who would like to take steps on a journey through the virtues that will build greater purpose in their life. It a purposeful choice to have a clear dream, vision, focus and plan, that will definitely bring lasting benefits to the person. Most people focus on their weakness, past failures, defeats, and disappointment. Some waste their energy on thinking about those who disappointed them or did not help them to achieve their desired objective. It is not the person who did something to obstruct you that is important but your heart. The enemy loves us to concentrate in hurts, pains, wrong suffered and offences.

Proverbs 4:23 (WEB) says, "Keep your heart with all diligence, for out of it is the wellspring of life." The mind is the doorway that the heart of an individual is under constant attack or what can be called continuous bombardment by the force of darkness. I love the verse in the word of God Proverb 4:23 (WEB), where it calls the heart the "wellspring of life. This means that it is the source of everything else in the life because from your heart overflows into thoughts, words, and actions. That is the reason it is especially important to guard your heart to avoid casualties in this mind war. The force of darkness can camouflage this attack that an individual involved in this situation may not even realize the reality of this war, although that does not present its existence.

The enemy like to obscure the truth from every one of us. The force of darkness is the father of lies and deception. There is no doubt that we have an adversary, who opposes God, everyone and everything that has a relationship with God. The goal of this adversary is to steal, kill and destroy. However, we have not been abandoned or neglected in a helpless situation. The Lord himself goes before you and will be with you; he will never leave you nor forsake you. Do not be afraid; do not be discouraged. Let us therefore come boldly unto the throne of grace, that we may obtain mercy, and find grace to help in time of need.

It is particularly important that you must be careful about nothing; but in everything by prayer and supplication with thanksgiving let your requests be made known unto God. The adversary may use all kinds of weapons, in the general format of circumstance or situations that leads to discouragement, disillusionment and disappointment with the aim to make you stop resisting and give up or surrender and quit. That is the reason, you must guard your heart more than anything else because the source of your life flows from it. It says the source of your life flows from your heart and not from someone. Your heart is your most important access to guard because it is extremely valuable, i.e., the source of everything you do.

In Mark chapter 11 verse 24 (NIV), says "Therefore I tell you, whatever you ask for in prayer, believe that you have received it, and it will be yours," Faith is of the heart, and there are times you can have faith in your heart but doubt in your head. That is the time to set your mind on the truth of the word of promise focusing on what matters most to you in this life, this is antidote to impatience, lack of perseverance, and certainly lack of peace of mind. Let the peace of Christ rule in your hearts since as a Christian you were called to peace.

The secret is to be thankful, being grateful for what is, always focusing on what is the most important goal, while taking every available opportunity to be generous, kind, forgiving in love and assisting others to climb the ladder of to their success. Prayer, which includes daily meditating in the word of God's promises for your situation will in cluster your mind to your specific need and taking the right decision will eliminate impatience, worry and anxiety. This is what the word says in Psalm chapter 84 verse 11 (NIV), "For the LORD God is a sun and shield; the LORD bestows favor and honor; no good thing does he withhold from those whose walk is blameless." If it is possible, as far as it depends on you, live at peace with everyone. As you meditate in the Word these verses should have your attention that the almighty God treat us with kindness and with honour, will not deny good thing to anyone who live right.

# *Plan To Succeed*

The scripture in Jeremiah chapter 29 verse 11 to 13 (NIV) says, "For I know the plans I have for you," declares the LORD, "plans to prosper you and not to harm you, plans to give you hope and a future. Then you will call on me and come and pray to me, and I will listen to you. You will seek me and find me when you seek me with all your heart." My friends in any moment of trials and difficulties in the journey of life, there is great comfort meditating in the Word of God. In the book of Jeremiah chapter 29 verse 11 continue to bless me knowing that it is not a quick fix promise from God, but rather a promise that the Almighty and all-knowing God has actually a plan for my life.

The good news is that God has also plan for everyone that will believe regardless of our race, nationality, challenges, and situation. This plan is the wisdom of God to give us prosperity, hope and a good future. What a great joy knowing that God's wisdom will always be available for us in every situation in life. God promises to be there for us in every moment of life or the situations we encounter in life. However, we are encouraged or commanded to play a role and that is "to call on God and come and pray to God… The almighty God will listen to us. We will seek God and find God when we seek God with all our heart."

For I know the plans I have for you," declares the Lord, "plans to prosper you and not to harm you, plans to give you hope and a future. We are commanded to have hope because the Word of God tells us that all things work for the good of those who love God, who have been called according to his purpose. They encouraged to live joyfully and successfully in the present, always having a dream of a better future and a plan to achieve our set goals. There is no room stagnancy, even in the event of a partial delay, but with wisdom always boldly moving forward with updated plan. Believing God in every moment will bring you out of trials and challenges into His greater plan, purpose, and blessing for your life. Jesus is made for us wisdom and we have access to the wisdom of God through the leadership of the Holy Spirit. What a great blessing we have in Christ Jesus.

2 Peter chapter 1 verse 1 to 3 (NIV) says "Simon Peter, a servant and apostle of Jesus Christ, To those who through the righteousness of our God and Savior Jesus Christ have received a faith as precious as ours: Grace and peace be yours in abundance through the knowledge of God and of Jesus our Lord. His divine power has given us everything we need for a godly life through our knowledge of him who called us by his own glory and goodness."

Through these God has given us his very great and precious promises, so that through them we may participate in the divine nature, having escaped the corruption in the world caused by evil desires.

My friends one of my greatest joy in life is that I am convinced or fully persuaded that God has a plan for us, and He has revealed it to us in His word. The Lord has abundant blessings for us His children in the Word. God has revealed to us that He has a plan for our lives, and it is our responsibility to seek and find out that plan through prayer and meditation. God may sometimes permit us to go through some situation in life that are hard and difficult. The good news is that God also has a plan to bring us victory by allowing it to bring greater hope, growth, and richer blessings, as part of His purpose and plan for our own lives. These experiences make us to be better person and blessing to other people. We can take credit ourselves for cooperating with His plan and purpose for our life always acknowledging the fact that the talents we have come from the master, Jesus Christ.

However, to achieve our desired dreams or goals in life, we either plan to succeed or you plan to fail. Although nobody in his [or her] her right mind will plan deliberately to fail in achieving an objective or reaching a goal, but if someone is having no written plan for success it is indirectly a plan not to succeed. That may not be your intention but that could be the ultimate result of a lack of plan. The almighty God has a plan for me, and His plan is exceptionally good, because He must has also given me the talent to succeed. That means I have a responsibility to find out that plan, write it down and seek the wisdom of God to use properly the talent He has given me to achieve successfully that plan.

The writing of the plan is absolutely important because you must have a purpose for your life, success comes from achieving that desired visions and planned goals. God has given everyone, the talent, value, and the wisdom to accomplish the purpose and plan for their lives. That is why it is so vital to know your gifts and talents whatever you do, and so that you can be successful in life. So, there is no room for making excuses, complaining or comparison. Anyone who really wants something good will do what it takes or find a way to go after that desire or dream. Every day we should expect to receive favour and acquire more knowledge to enable us to go through our plans and purpose for that day.

We should seek guidance, strength, and direction of the holy Spirit, while having a daily routine that motivates us to work hard on ourselves. However, we must be willing to keep educating ourselves to face the various challenges ahead, so that they could become steppingstone instead of hindrance. Faith takes the daily rich blessings gifts from God almighty faithful hands that never fails to supply our needs according to His abundance riches. Having a vision without a follow-up plan is not appropriate, because success means the achievement of planned goals. Sometimes, others are involved in whatever you have achieved, and when the outcome enables other people to have better and more advanced life, is considered a success that bless. The making of various plan short, middle, and long-term plans which could be from one year to several years, is one of the recommended things that you do for goal setting.

# *Patience*

Philippians chapter 4 verse 6 (NIV), says "Do not be anxious about anything, but in every situation, by prayer and petition, with thanksgiving, present your requests to God." The word of God encourages us not be anxious about anything, but in every situation, by prayer and petition, with thanksgiving, present your requests to God. We are commanded that when we ask, we must believe and not doubt, because the one who doubts is like a wave of the sea, blown and tossed by the wind. How do we keep our focus after making our requests in prayers and how can we keep from doubt and most especially from worrying? My anchor verses that help me to be patience and believing to receive with joys, before it is actually accomplish in real life what have been visualizing for years are Matthew chapter 21 verse 22 (NIV), which says "If you believe, you will receive WHATEVER YOU ASK FOR IN PRAYER."

I believe because God is able to do exceedingly above all that I ask for in prayers. The other verse that gives me patience to the challenge to staying in faith, so as to receive what is visualized and put on the vision tablet to happen at the appointed time is the scripture from the book of Isaiah 28 verse 16 (KJV) "Therefore thus saith the Lord GOD, Behold, I lay in Zion for a foundation a stone, a tried stone, a precious corner *stone*, a sure foundation: he that believeth shall not make haste." Therefore, for what is visualized and put on the vision tablet to happen at the appointed time, which is a sure foundation of your belief you shall not make haste or doubt for it will surely come to pass if you maintain focus. To live according to your desired plan and to walk in your vision is great but the vision or dream God placed in your heart, and you see with the eyes of faith giving to you in the light of God's grace will be confronted by darkness forces, that is challenges, trials, obstacles will come against you and try to prevent you from accomplishing those goals at the appointed time. The real fight is the elapsed time between the vision and the accomplishment or more precisely the time you believe and the time you receive.

That is where we need the great gift that not highly proclaimed but very essential. I am talking about Patience in your faith work. Patience is a virtue that must be cherished and desired by everyone who loves success. Most successful have probably failed many times before they became remarkably successful. Patience enables you to keep focus, keep at it until you become the master. Patience is the spirit that conquer, that does not give up easily, that is not easily discourage, that encourages himself even in the event of a partial or temporary failure. Patience does not find faults with others but looks deep into self and fights to improve the dream with the next best effort. Patience builds in you the spirit of diligent and resilient. They accept mistakes and seek to solution.

Every successful person knows what a wonderful gift God has given to mankind to be able to withstand or recover quickly from difficult conditions. The beauty of resilience is the understanding that life is full of challenges, but I can overcome the obstacles through Christ who strengthen me. The power of self-reliant and resilient through patience will bring the vision or goal to pass at an appointed time or date. The story of soccer plays staying behind after the team normal hours of training to practice the "free kicks", "penalty kicks" alone, musician practicing on the keyboard, drums, guitar, tennis players, authors, actors, students studying to solve the mathematics or other materials to overcome the challenges, struggle to improve, to develop the gift and fulfil the goal that we are more than a conqueror through the gift in us by Christ Jesus.

My friend, God is so good and has given to every mankind everything we need and will ever need for a good life. In 2 Peter chapter 1 verse 3 to 4 (NLT), "By his divine power, God has given us everything we need for living a godly life. We have received all of this by coming to know him, the one who called us to himself by means of his marvellous glory and excellence." A person of patience has the resilient to maintain control of a situation and seek new methods to solve or overcome difficulties, obstacles, or problems. Good things come to those who wait on the Lord. People who are in haste to achieve quick success without facing challenges, that is "fast tracks" always lead in most cases to a wasted life.

Anything that is good is worth waiting for in patience by overcoming the various difficulties and problems on the road to success. The book of Ecclesiastes chapter 3 verse 1 (NIV) says that There is a time for everything, and a season for every activity under the heavens. I cannot change the season and I do not know if you can, but I can change by the power of the Holy Spirit. There are always on the road to success the temptation to quit after a partial failure, a major obstacle, challenges, and setbacks but do not unless you are completely certain that all available options have all failed, because the trying of your faith worketh patience.

James chapter 1 verses 2 to 9 (NIV), says, "Consider it pure joy, my brothers and sisters, whenever you face trials of many kinds, ³because you know that the testing of your faith produces perseverance. Let perseverance finish its work so that you may be mature and complete, not lacking anything. If any of you lacks wisdom, you should ask God, who gives generously to all without finding fault, and it will be given to you. But when you ask, you must believe and not doubt, because the one who doubts is like a wave of the sea, blown and tossed by the wind. That person should not expect to receive anything from the Lord. Such a person is double-minded and unstable in all they do. Believers in humble circumstances ought to take pride in their high position."

Let have a quick glance at the life of some of the successful people in the bible who had patience to wait for the expected promise. Caleb son of Jephunneh at the age of 85 years told Joshua, now give me this hill country that the LORD promised me that day and his uncompromising patience was crowned with success for then Joshua blessed Caleb son of Jephunneh and gave him Hebron as his inheritance. Jacob had to work patiently for fourteen years, in his uncle's business before he could marry Rachel the woman he loved, instead of the already difficult seven years agreement because Laban gave him for a wife her elder daughter Leah in a trick wedding.

Patience while you are waiting is the real test of your faith because the delay could be due to opposition or simply having to wait longer than planned date. David trusting God deeply while waiting for about twenty years to become the greatest king in the history of Israel. How about the story of Joseph's growth, developing patience and maturity for thirteen years, as a seventeen-year-old slave boy and later prison sentence for an offence he did not commit in a foreign land before becoming the prime minister. The mind/set is particularly important to remain patience and not becoming anxious when dealing with problems or difficult situations. This could also mean giving your attention to something for a long time without becoming discouraged or completely losing interest.

Once again, my friend, we all cherish success but the road to success is growth in character because which comes as we develop patience which is a virtue. In this journey you are bound to have various phases which are testing, going through times of road bumps, roadblocks, "slow men at work", trials, and even suffering, without getting angry, upset, and frustrated. It involves trusting God and the talent and dream given to you that things will happen at the appointed time. Your mindset will determine how you behave based on your life principles whether they are right and wrong.

Your determination to behave in a way that shows the goodness of your rugged character will either make you or break you. That is the simple reason behind the biblical statement that says, "patience is a virtue!" A person of virtue is someone behaving in a way that shows the goodness of his [or her] character. Therefore, a person of virtue has a "behaviour demonstrating high moral standards." While moral means simply to be "concerned with the principles of right and wrong behaviour and the goodness or badness of human character." So, patience demonstrates the right behaviour and the goodness of a person's character.

He that believed shall not be in haste. Having a plan with your desired vision or goal is the foundation of success. However, there are times in your life you may want something to change immediately or that you are not willing to wait for the appropriate time of the vision or set goals. This brings to my mind the story of the farmer who planted seeds that he knows very well it takes time to come to maturity but wants it immediately. I had to deal with this frustrating urgency to have something before maturity.

Is that why you are in such a hurry.? Do you always want it immediately or you are prepared to wait for the appropriate time? The worst scenario is expecting to succeed without any plan. I think lack of plan to succeed is a plan to fail completely. Why did I say complete failure or fail completely because when you have a plan, partial failure or some minor failures can be corrected as you go along the journey of success. Some minor failure should not be an obstacle but a "self-motivating" tonic to do better and better, until the desired goal is achieved.

The important of planning enables us to have a "scale of preference" or "priority list." Trying to get too many things done at the same is not always wise, it is better to concentrate at one event at a time for success. However, there are occasions when you do two tasks at the same time or some form of multitasking if it is thoughtfully planned and executed. Most people tend to lose their patience when they are multitasking or when they are on a tight schedule. There should always be in any plan some form of "contingency plan" or "plan B". Some form of flexibility in the event of obstacles or setbacks which enables a replanning or reschedule. This will eliminate stress, worry and obviously impatience.

Impatience can destroy creativity, motivation, interest, and concentration or focus. One thing to keep in mind is that you do not want to lose is focus. Your eyes and your mind must be set on the goals or vision. This is always the initial suggestion anytime you are over stretching yourself too thin, take a pause, be calm, have a rethink or reconsider your daily, weekly, monthly plan or if you do not have a plan check your to-do list. If you do not have a plan, schedule, timeline, or to-do list simply create one immediately.

The first human instinct is always a wrong attempt to change our natural reaction to the situation, or circumstances that is overwhelming. This should be checked by exercising self-control. Then take the steps to have a deeper look at the plan or to-do list and rescheduled your tasks properly so as to enable you to do only one thing at a time in case there are tasks to be done by external parties, delegate properly responsibilities and re-visit your schedule daily to eliminate impatience by addressing delay, difficulties, and setbacks. However, remember, your plan or to-do list cannot foresee all risks, so even the mitigation or contingency plan has its limitation, so be patience with yourself and work daily on your plan or to-do list.

There are certain issues that needs to be addressed in the case of a person that is always impatience. The issue is to address the factors that can often contribute for a person to lose patience. In this case we are looking into the aspect of setting personal goals and the issues of life.

The fact that we have goals and believing to accomplish our desire does not indicate there will not be storms. Mitigation helps in reducing the seriousness, painfulness, or severity such an event. However, the storms that could come against you, are not meant to keep you down. They are meant to lift you to a higher level, to promote, or accelerate your success.

Those who hope in the Lord will renew their strength. They will soar on wings like eagles; they will run and not grow weary; they will walk and not be faint. Most people know that the eagle uses the winds of the storm to rise and be lifted higher. The correlation is that the storms in our lives, also can be an opportunity to renew our strength, so that we can use it to lift us to greater heights of achievements or success. When impatience occurs, you become worried, very anxious, unhappy, and sometimes angry. The reasons for these feelings of impatience may not be so, apparent, or plain because you may not clearly see the presence of visible signs that leads to your sad countenance.

A merry heart makes a cheerful countenance: but by sorrow of the heart the spirit is broken. Those around you may equally not understand the presence of visible signs that leads to your sad countenance and cannot encourage you, even if they desire because Iron sharpened iron; so, a man sharpened the countenance of his friend. In the book of Nehemiah chapter 2 verse 2 (NIV) says, "so the king asked me, "Why does your face look so sad when you are not ill? This can be nothing but sadness of heart."

The word of God says, God makes a way where there seems to be no way. It is of utmost importance to realise and be aware of the root cause of lack of patience and address it. The essential thing to do is to take an inventory of your life. Have a deeper look at your current mind-set, vision, goals or to-do-list, family, relations, friends, how you spend your time or days, words (spoken

and writing), situations and circumstances that could influence or cause you frustration, distress, anxiety, unnecessary stress, and worry. Growth will only happen if you are aware of the root cause for your impatience because you cannot grow unless you find out the issue, take responsibility by acknowledging if the helpful or damaging, take action to deal with it, and learn something from such an experience, because victory over impatience is having the power to change to be a better person.

A lasting success will demand a change in your attitude about life because progress comes by daily routine or learning and training your mind, on purpose to having the right mind-set. This will take daily meditation in the word of God. This should be one of the first things to do daily in the morning. Patience is essential to accomplish your desires and to be successful in life, so you must start each day to prepare your mind. The word of God has the power to help us have the right mindset, because the light comes in and expels darkness, the eye of your understanding is opened because you are able to see what God sees in you and you are able to receive God's truths that brings hope, faith, and encouragement to patiently overcome the storm.

There are some situation that you cannot do anything about to change, situations that you simply cannot resolve and instead of being impatience, you just learn to give the burden to the Lord, saying this praying "Lord I know you can help me, give me the grace to be patience and I commit the situation into your hands knowing you will never leave me nor forsake" Hebrews chapter 4 verse 16 (NIV) says it this way, " Let us then approach God's throne of grace with confidence, so that we may receive mercy and find grace to help us in our time of need." This an invitation to accept wisely although you may sometimes find it difficult to let go but it must be done to alleviate impatience and avoid the serious consequence. It is our responsibility to make a determined effort to grow and develop in our "inner man" in the power of God's might, to remain patient even in the testing, trying and enduring situations of life.

Have an appropriate plans or to-do-list and follow it with discipline but do not insist on getting all things done immediately or beyond your faith. Do not over stretch your faith, rather grow in faith. Avoid shipwreck because your faith and thoughts are connected, so cling to or do not give up and do not let go of your faith because you can do all things through Christ who is your strength. The Holy Scripture in 1 Timothy chapter 1 verse 19 (NIV), says "holding on to faith and a good conscience, which some have rejected and so have suffered shipwreck with regard to the faith." Always keep in mind that a lasting full joy is better than immediate partial gratification and remember to rejoice always and do not lose your patience because most thing that are good in life take time, self-discipline, rugged determination and sometimes the good fight of faith will be required to fight the giant that wants to prevent you from getting to the next level of your success. The people who are impatient, sometimes are more likely to give up on things that are important to them at the edge of their breakthrough.

My friends, I agree with you that good things may not always come immediately but trusting God, they do come to those who will not give up easily on their vision and set goals. Growth in wisdom, knowledge and understanding and maturity in patience help us to be aware that we will eventually get the strong desire of your heart. Success does not come cheap, so it will demands working hard at your vision, keep your focus on your goals, enjoy little successes in your journey and recognize that the things you desire others may have it easier than you.

The fact is that you are not in race with you friends or anybody, the things that matter to you are your focus, having the right mind-set and whatever happens, do not compare yourself with others, never, and I repeat never, because negative comparison will suck life out a person. This will certainly lead to frustration, low self-esteem, in most of the cases you may become impatient with your-self. It is good to learn from others and to desire to be successful as others and be in the company of those who are successful, but their achievements should motivate us or challenge us to do better. Life is a journey and not a race between you and your pairs. The secret of patience can be found in having a positive outlook, enjoying life day by day and admiring your progress. Taking every step with appreciation and avoiding unnecessary comparison will eliminate impatience.

My friend every successful person has had disappointments, failures some form of attacks, major storms, and probably a moment wanting abandon or to give-up. Psalm chapter 127 verse 1 and 2 (NIV) says, "Unless the LORD builds the house, the builders labor in vain. Unless the LORD watches over the city, the guards stand watch in vain. In vain you rise early and stay up late, toiling for food to eat - for he grants sleep to those he loves." The secret is rest taking time to sit quietly and think of the good things done and taking your eyes off your mistakes, failures, and disappointments. Return to your rest, my soul, for the Lord has been good to you. The good news about rest is that taking some time out, you develop the mind-set and attitude necessary to be more patience with yourself.

The road to success is a challenge that does not always run smoothly but full of bumps, failures, attacks and maybe storms. Be determined to get to the other side where success is waiting to embrace you. Appreciate life while you are resting, as a good opportunity to do nothing but to recharge your energy. A moment to be grateful and excited looking forward to another updated plan to reinvest your time and talent. In other words, stay focused in the storm. It is meant to lift you to a higher level if you maintain the right mindset and attitude. The mind-set is particularly important, having a renewed in your attitude that you can be patient no matter the difficulties and it will propel you to accomplish your goals.

This is an area where meditation will help you to be more patience. Patient with yourself means you love, respect, believe in the ability that is you and eventually your effort will lead you to success. Failure is common to everyone but the determination, passion, or motivation to succeed is what makes the difference in every situation, in the drive to achieve your dream. This is not a suggestion that you do not have patience because you lack passion, or motivation but the fact that depending on the situation or circumstances your patience may varies, so it is not always easy to develop patience, so for any situation you have got to be motivated to become more patient.

One of my motivation or meditation scriptures to maintain patience in the event of a partial failure is found in Philippians chapter 4 verse 13 (NIV), "I can do all this through him who gives me strength." Trusting Jesus and the wisdom given to you will lead you to succeed, the common factor is that most successful people have faced various challenges and have failed over and over again, over and over again, so many times without given up and that is one of the secrets or reasons for their success. This is where you must set-your-mind not to quit and most specially to resist the temptation of comfort and convenience zones that leads to unsuccessful lifestyle.

It is not always easy to put in the extra effort in the event of a partial failure, lack of fast break or immediate success to encourage you to move to the next level. That is really the test that brings the best in you. That extra push in the mist of obstacle or challenges makes the difference between ordinary and extraordinary person. The ability to face the challenge with a smile in the midst of a storm without getting angry or frustrated. The ability to be calm and maintain focus in the mist of opposition and various criticisms. Patience is power in disguise, the ability to be on course in the event of a storm while others are criticizing, without distraction you are still on it, and while others are quitting you are using it as a steppingstone.

Patience gives you power to be on course and still thinking of how to overcome the next mountain, so that you can move to a higher level of success. Sometimes, when you are getting ready to go to a new level, the next level of your life, it is not always a move from a difficult zone but also to vacate a comfort zone. As a matter of fact, the issue is not the condition of the zone, but the state of your mindset, you must make the right choice and be boldly determined to go for what is the best for your life without stricken back in fear and insecurity. Patience brings the best in you, using challenges as steppingstone to your next level. Faith receives it but its patience that takes or possess it. The goal is yours for taking and to possess with patience. Success does not come easily but comes through the amount of excellence doing what is over and above developed with patience.

## The Danger of Impatience

The ability to acknowledge your limits and accepting your weakness without allowing it to discourage or annoy you will become easier with time, so in the meantime you must learn or practice patience or else it will hinder your success. This discouragement will make things more difficult and, in some cases, even make the situation worse, which is the opposite of what you desire. Some people make their situation worse by getting annoyed and angry with themselves, for the situation or blame someone for the problem. Looking at the negative situation and becoming impatience can increase your stress levels and steal your joy, peace, and happiness which can only makes things worse. The best thing to do is to stop focusing on the negative situation and start thinking positively, this is as good as it gets. Remember always, you must see something before you can have something. This will reduce your stress levels and improve your concentration.

When you focused on the solution, and your ability to acknowledge something without allowing it to steal your peace and joy, the solution with time will become easier. Angry with yourself or somebody about the problem will only increase your unhappiness and a step backward from the solution. The way out is to document the issues that causes the problem meditate properly over it and plan solution with efforts, dates, and time. Patience is a virtue, strength and an anchor of faith which means that you are strong have the ability and grown in maturity to hold back, control or govern your predisposition to emotions like sadness, fear, anxiety, and anger. Patience is largely about enduring something and controlling your emotions. The power to govern these emotions will lead to better knowledge, understanding and courage to overcome the difficulties.

Patience is not easy because sometimes, we do not like to wait, that the reason it is worthwhile to cultivate. What makes patience annoying is that it is contrary to our normal instincts, having something immediately, instead of the desire to wait for it at the appropriate day and time. Impatient people are like little children who plant seeds in the morning and expects it immediately to grow to a tree in the evening. Though it would be nice to be able to pluck fruits the same day but that is not always the case because the day you plant the seed is not always the day you eat the fruit.

Every good seed we plant in life will always take time to come to maturity. The moment you make up your mind that you are going to plant good seeds in your life, to do certain things for your progress, the Holy Spirit will empower you but also you become a threat to the forces of darkness. There will be pressure and you will go through attacks to stop you from following through with your desire. If you trust God and patiently collaborate with Him for the plan, it is only going to make you fruitful. So, the pressure is going to propel you out of the storm and into your destiny.

In fact, let me tell you, my friend never you make a permanent decision on temporary feelings especially in the moment of storm because you are responsible for your life choices and decisions, whether good or bad. Patience in the moment of storm will cause you to be perceived as mightier than you are because you do not know if the situation is going to take you out or take you over, that is exactly when and where your faith begins to flourish. When the roads before you are not noticeably clear and the future success seems dim, do not get impatient? Do you get frustrated for not knowing sometimes? Are you courageous to confront the challenges and trusting the Lord to guide you with wisdom? Are you confidently revisiting and adjusting your plans, taking the necessary steps to accomplish your dream future? That is some of the questions you need to ask yourself. Some self-searching questions.

Many successful people have failed so many times without given-up their hope and dreams, and eventually their tenacity paid-off with outstanding success. The main war in won or lost in the mind. If you have a negative or a "grasshopper" mindset you will fail but you can change your mindset to understand that the storm you are facing is preparing you for the next level. The storm is a steppingstone and not a hindrance. What if you could not reach your destiny without it? Right from childhood some of us read the Bible story of David and Goliath. He built his strength in the farm when nobody was watching him pulling out the lamp from the lion's mouth. If it were not for Goliath, he would still be known as a shepherd boy. He prepared diligently, disciplined and when Goliath was placed in his path, not to defeat him but to promote him.

These issues you are confronting today, may seems like a setback, but it is really a setup to promote you. So, when you overcome this obstacle, you will step up to another level. So, set-your-mind on a higher level and not on the problem. It will take discipline making plans to achieve your goals and daily revisiting your plans while others are either daydreaming or not preparing but indirectly are making plans to fail. It will take discipline to study while others are watching television. It will take discipline yourself taking and acting on your decision while others are procrastinating or giving excuses. It will take discipline, to spend money and use your time wisely while others wasting their money and previous time.

The good thing about discipline is that though it may seem not comfortable, when you make the decision to become a person of discipline, the benefits are enormous. If you will not allow the pressure to convince you to quit, it is going to require complete commitment to yourself. Successful people do more than what is expected of them most of the time. In fact, it will be normal for you to do what is expected of you, because success comes by doing more and more than what is required by everyone. The spirit of excellence in a person makes him [or her] do what is required over and above and that determines increase in greatness. The scripture says, in Psalm chapter 71 verse 21 (NIV), "You will increase my honor and comfort me once more."

Most of the time it hard to wait specially to become a discipline person because it certainly demands a lot of self-control. Difficulties and trials bring strength and growth that leads to greatness. Most of us, if we will admit it have been guilty of wanting things to happen in our time, that is "now time." The world moves in a "fast lane", always in a hurry. The challenges and trials of life must have immediate solution, they must come to a stop, preferably exchanged for complete comfort. These challenges should not make anyone who desire success feel unqualified, and uncomfortable, but should drive us to go the extra mile to do better.

There is power within that can assist us in our weakness, but we must play our part. We must resist the temptation to be worried, sad, or even loose hope. We must wait patiently for the Lord, because God's time could be different but always much better. The difference between ordinary and extraordinary is a choice of immediate comfort and convenience or more applying extra effort to do beyond the ordinary. This takes strong faith trusting God that good thing will happen at the appropriate time, and requires going through hard times, without getting up-set about the situation.

The danger of being impatient is that you may lose your focus on your long-term goals, because to become a person excellent spirit patience will enable you to develop the "back-bone" for a successful lifestyle. Everyone should strive for a reputation for an admirable persistence. The fact that you are so persistent and never gave up trying to get or achieve your good dreams or vision always has its rewards because in due season you will reap if you faint not in your mind. Most successful people have failed many times before achieving their goals. The sky is not the limit but your faith. Is that not a good reason patience is a virtue? Listen, my friend patience is not always the easiest thing to do but its long-term benefits are massive, it has great rewards. In addition to an exceptionally good reputation, you will definitely enjoy a prosperous mental and physical healthy lifestyle that others will admire.

Romans chapter 8 verse 24 to 25 (NIV), "[24] For in this hope we were saved. But hope that is seen is no hope at all. Who hopes for what they already have? [25] But if we hope for what we do not yet have, we wait for it patiently." When we exercise patience with other people, it is an expression of love and kindness. It helps to build healthy relationships. The benefits of being patient is building lasting and joyful friendships, in our business, romance, and family relationships. We can learn to be more patience. The starting point of patience is personal, peace within me and family members before practicing patience with other people. If we do not have patience with ourselves, we would not have insight into their problems or some challenges they are going through in life.

Practicing Patience is a choice we make in our life to have a healthy relationship. Patience brings about the best for us, to be kind and loving to other people, even in the event of difficulties and strong challenges. It builds strength in our lives in the time of storm, to accomplish successful our goals and objectives. Most people who are privilege to have relationship with someone who is patience will tell you how grateful they are to be so blessed of such a relationship with the man or [woman] having such a unusual and surprising amount of patience with them. The scripture says in Colossian chapter 2 verse 10 (NIV), "and in Christ you have been brought to fullness. He is the head over every power and authority."

Every person should be allowed to be human and be seen as a whole person, with human flaws. We all love someone who is patient with us. People are grateful and cherish those who accepts their limitations and does not hold them to an impossible standard. There are awesome joy and satisfaction when we patience is expressed in our friendship. Long lasting friendship is born from practicing patience with one another. Most people will tell you that a good reason for their exceptionally good friendship for such a long-time is because they have learnt to practice patience with one another. Patience never gives up on one another because is full of love and kindness.

I remember a particular situation about this particular fellow who was a co-manager on a project. His was a very bright and intelligent man but exceedingly difficult to work with him, because he was always irritated and had no patience with fellow colleagues. He could not tolerate any mistake or flaws in the life of other people. We cannot express how grateful we are for colleagues and friends over these past years who through patience and gentleness has been one of the great constants of our lives.

Proverbs chapter 16 verse 32 (NIV), says, "Better a patient person than a warrior, one with self-control than one who takes a city." Developing the gift of patience is much like practicing self-control, taking decision to calm down in the heat of the moment, even in the event of challenging circumstances, most especially when things do not go your way. Some people simply fail to relax and put an issue in proper perspective. I have seen people fuss and get impatience over things which within the frame of the whole picture or in a period of a month either means little, does not matter, or add no substantial value to the matter in question. In some cases, this show of worries, anger, or unnecessary impatience, greater than the situations deserves demonstrates weakness in character.

Proverbs chapter 14 verse 29 (NIV) says, "Whoever is patient has great understanding, but one who is quick-tempered displays folly." This previous gift, patience is a virtue that does not come easily to everyone, although we all have the potential to be patient. Practicing patient, demands a great deal of hard work that takes committed time, a whole lot of self-disciplined effort, self-control, and persistence. Some people that are indiscipline procrastinate and they mistakenly think that is exercising patience. That is false patience which could lead to frustration. A person that has a vision and a defined plan to realize the desired good dreams, does not procrastinate but take discipline, commitment, and actions to achieve the set goals and objectives, sometimes it could involve doing much more than the ordinary and most especially getting outside the so-called comfort zone.

The scripture says, in Galatians chapter 5 verse 22 to 23 (NIV), "But the fruit of the Spirit is love, joy, peace, forbearance, kindness, goodness, faithfulness, gentleness and self-control. Against such things there is no law." These are fruit of the Holy Spirit in the life of a child of God. These traits can only be developed with the help of the Holy Spirit. They are God given virtues that are given to us during the new birth. These virtues love, joy, peace, patience, kindness, goodness, faithfulness, gentleness, and self-control are often contrary to our human nature, but produce long term gains and are very essential for living your best life. These are fruit of the Holy Spirit in the life of a child of God. They are God given virtues that are given to us during the new birth.

These virtues help us to develop our faith, self-confidence and live a more meaningful life. It is he abundant life everyone desire, walking daily in the goodness and blessed which is the pleasant life dream. A life where everyone is treated with love, respect, and sincere kindness. It brings joy, peace, and unity into friendship and relationship. A more meaningful life, full of confidence and boldness which comes out of cultivating the spirit of patience. This certainly makes life much more pleasant and full of joy. People of patience have good respect for themselves, and they treat others with kindness and respect. They add value to other people's lives and even go a long way to satisfy others, creating a healthy relationship.

Their presence brings satisfaction, peace, and joy into relationship, at work, friends, and the family. They are joy bringers, a character that brings unity among friends and within family members. With patience they help to improve the life of everyone around, and this leads to happier lives and healthier relationship. It is a decision to practice and improve on our self and be a better person. Growing in patience is not learning a new habit but connecting into the socket of the fruit of the spirit and continuing that habit time after time until it becomes a part of your normal lifestyle. The fruit of the Spirit represents the outward or visible growth believers experience in Christ through the Holy Spirit.

Patience like love, kindness, gentleness "fruit of the spirit" Galatians chapter 5 verse 22-23 (NIV). "But the fruit of the Spirit is love, joy, peace, forbearance, kindness, goodness, faithfulness, gentleness and self-control. Against such things there is no law."

This is a gift of the Holy Spirit rather than a decision to be committed to the wellbeing of others without any conditions or circumstances. When you intentionally decide to live and walk in these habits, you are open to a more meaningful, healthier lifestyle with better opportunities, truly walking in the light of the person God created you to be and live. However, for some people patience is a skill that you have to learn and practice. It helps build our reputations for persistence and improves our relationships with all those around us. we do not always have all the answers to life questions because we are called to continuous learning and growth through challenges in the journey of life. Those who are matured in patience as a lifestyle enjoy, peace and unity in the family.

## The Test of Patience

The scripture says in Matthew chapter 7 verse 24 to 27 (NIV) "Therefore everyone who hears these words of mine and puts them into practice is like a wise man who built his house on the rock. The rain came down, the streams rose, and the winds blew and beat against that house; yet it did not fall, because it had its foundation on the rock. But everyone who hears these words of mine and does not put them into practice is like a foolish man who built his house on sand. The rain came down, the streams rose, and the winds blew and beat against that house, and it fell with a great crash."

The only way to know if you have patience, is storm. So, what can you do when your patience is tried or tested by challenges? In your Christian walk of faith, you will go through some tough times, but remember storms never last forever. In the midst of the storm, we run to the Lord and look to God for help and shelter.

The book of James chapter 1 verse 2 to 5 (NIV), says, "Consider it pure joy, my brothers and sisters, whenever you face trials of many kinds, because you know that the testing of your faith produces perseverance. Let perseverance finish its work so that you may be mature and complete, not lacking anything. If any of you lacks wisdom, you should ask God, who gives generously to all without finding fault, and it will be given to you."

In the journey of life unexpected act of nature could prevent our plans from happening smoothly. Live curves are not always accompanied with a pre-warning road-sign. There are some unexpected storms that could deliberately cause a problem to damage or change the goals of a person in a way that ruins it. In some cases, it could actually prevent it from working properly. Here is where the virtue of patience is demonstrated. The place to develop this kind of patience is prayer and meditation.

There are different kinds of meditations practiced all over the world, but to be specific a session of biblical meditation is what you need to increase your patience when you noticed that it is low. Faith comes from hearing and hearing the Word of God, while patience comes from developing the fruits of the Holy Spirit through meditation in the Word. During trying times, we must turn to God, through meditation and prayer for guidance. When we are exhausted and tempted to be worried, finding patience is pathway to a healthy lifestyle.

## Taking Control of Impatience

The book of Proverbs chapter 21 verse 15 (NIV) says "The plans of the diligent lead to profit as surely as haste leads to poverty." Richness in life is not always about what you accomplish within a certain time frame. In this world culture of hasting always to meet the deadline, competition driven, and ego motivated. This leads to frustration when you try to achieve goals at the expense of joy. Those who are ego motivates, will find themselves not happy or enjoying the goals they are trying to achieve. They are always sad and will never be as happy as the people who are purpose motivated. Patience will help you to reflect on your purpose and feel better about yourself which eventually will make you more pleasant to be around for others.

Meditation in the Word can also help you to figure out which things are more important in your life and teach you how to better practice patience. This will enable you to maintain focus or re-focus, if you have lost your focus on the goals that brings a sense of relaxation which improves the quality of your joy and satisfaction eliminating the feelings of frustration, worry anger and sadness. The best advice is be prepared for surprises or unplanned event or situations. The solution to be flexible but not procrastinate. Plan are made to be daily, weekly, monthly monitored and updated if and when necessary. The key words are focus and discipline; keep your eyes on the goal and make sure the delay is not due to indiscipline or lack of motivation. As much as you can avoid repeated neglect and carelessness, in your daily project tasks. Everyone who has an ever drawn up a project plan knows that there are always contingencies. There are some thresholds that can be avoided but there are also some events that you cannot foresee in your plan, so expect form of unexpected events or situations.

Be prepared to adjust and do not lose control because of impatience. Even when you have plans, certain things there are going to be always certain things that does not work out as planned. There could be a twist in the tail, be patient to always accept the twist and turns in life confidently. The best way to confront such difficulty circumstances is to keep your focus and always remember that you cannot plan against all avert situations. Some circumstances and the behaviour of everyone around you, could cause you to make some changes to your original plan and being impatience will only make it worse or complicated.

Psalms chapter 40 verse 1 (NIV) says, "I waited patiently for the Lord; he turned to me and heard my cry." These circumstances should not be a hindrance but steppingstone to growth and success. It is actual possible to eliminate whatever is responsible for that feeling associated with impatience. The first step is become more aware of it and be more prepared for the feeling of impatience. Then begin to take control of that circumstances surrounding the feeling. You will discover that you will be able to better control impatience when the feeling comes to you. Friends, my prayer for you is that may you be strengthened with all power, according to his glorious might, for all endurance and patience with joy, giving thanks to the Father, who has qualified you to share in the inheritance of the saints in light.

# Perseverance

Perseverance can be defined as the continued effort to do or achieve something despite difficulties, failure, or opposition. That said it all, but I would like to highlight or as some would say underline these words "Continued-effort" and "to-do" and "despite-difficulties", An abandoned idea is abandoned hope and abandoned hope is abandoned dream or goal. Keeping your hope and dream alive comes from having the right mid-set. I determinately make up my mind before the kick-off of the project that challenges will not stop me. Having a mind-set to move on despite the difficulties is especially important because some storms are inevitable. They also come uninvited and without any pre-view notification.

Therefore, perseverance is the ability to keep doing something in spite of obstacles. This is one of the most powerful traits to accomplish your good dream. The key is "self-accountability". Learn to be hold yourself accountable for your action. Make personal plans and promises and set up your mind to keep them. Determine to maintain the promises you make to yourself is vital to perseverance. Simply said is "your word good to you"? Do you believe yourself? If you promise yourself to act on a particular objective, small or large, are you confident to keep your promise to yourself or does your conscience witness to you that you cannot do it? This is actually amazingly easy to detect, simply take note of your previous goals and have a check of all your personal accountability records of various promises you made to yourself and then track how many you were able to accomplish successfully.

The ability to followed through with your promise despite difficulties is an evidence of your state of perseverance. This is crystal clear, because the people who persevere show steadfastness in doing something despite how hard it is or how long it takes to reach the goal. The good news is that you do not have to be the most brilliant person or genius to succeed because if you persevere, you can reach your goals. Growing up in a supported environment that permits you to experience failure or setbacks as a steppingstone to achieve your goals will definitely serve as an inspiration to always persevere.

The muscle is developed patiently by routine exercising, so also is perseverance, thinking your way through any challenge, and trying patiently again and again, until you develop the skill to convert setbacks to setup for success. That is, you take all the necessary steps to carry out your objectives in spite of difficulties. Whatever are your goals in life, this skill is fundamental to every success, so it is of utmost importance developing this gift or growing in this area, if you desire to achieve your plan or dreams in life. Perseverance will help you to be successful in life, whatsoever are those goals or the obstacles you encounter on the way. It is the inbuilt resilient from the kindergarten playing games with school mates to brainstorming with business partners in life. This virtue builds in every person still ruggedness to confront adversity with head held high. It gives in-built will power not to despair or give-up but rather strength to overcome temptation to quit, and to keep focus. The ability to keep moving forward against many mountainous obstacles, to achieve our goals.

Perseverance is that uncommon determination to continue in your plan with a faithful and consistent action of belief that occurs over a long period of time, notwithstanding the difficult challenges. Believers are encouraged to endure many trials, tribulations, persecution, and tests in the journey of life. They must not give-up, but steadfastly continue in their faith in God, and the strength of their faith propel them to endure hardship and become victorious. Trials reveal and test the deeper parts of our hearts. They bring to the light the true anchor of our souls. The object of faith for every believer is our Lord saviour Jesus Christ, and that is also the strength of our faith and our virtue to endure. For in him we live and move and have our being. As some of your own poets have said, we are his offspring. That is the reason we can rejoice in difficulties because in Christ, we are secured and fully convinced that our initial suffering produces endurance.

As it is written in Romans chapter 5 verse 3 to 5 (NIV), "Not only so, but we also glory in our sufferings, because we know that suffering produces perseverance; perseverance, character; and character, hope. And hope does not put us to shame, because God's love has been poured out into our hearts through the Holy Spirit, who has been given to us." The truth of the matter is there will be times that we will face serious challenges as Christians, and it is wrong to think that we will not. "Challenges produces Perseverance;" "Perseverance builds Character;" and "Character produces Hope."

Hope means you are placing your trust or faith on something positive to happen and you are not passive but taking the right action, to see that the outcome is successful. That means you are taking the right decision and working towards your desired goals with determination and diligence until your goals are accomplished successfully. Blessed is the one who perseveres under trial because, having stood the test, that person will receive the crown of life that the Lord has promised to those who love him. This virtue perseverance is what builds strong character, a closer relationship, and a success ladder to overcome various challenges in life.

Our attitude to challenges should be Philippians chapter 4 verse 4 through 7 (NIV), "Rejoice in the Lord always. I will say it again: Rejoice! Let your gentleness be evident to all. The Lord is near. Do not be anxious about anything, but in every situation, by prayer and petition, with thanksgiving, present your requests to God. And the peace of God, which transcends all understanding, will guard your hearts and your minds in Christ Jesus." Those of us who are Christians should grow in our knowledge of the wisdom and prosperity of God's love for us, and our minds should be renewed in the word of God and our spirits develop a restful faith of the power, love, and grace of God.

We must always remember that God will make all things work together for our good and that His purposes will be achieved. Our Lord is a shield around us; our glory, the one who holds our heads high. I am not suggesting it is easy, because success does not fall on you like a bed of roses by doing nothing on your own part, because you have a major role to play, however we cannot deny the fact that patience and perseverance during hard seasons enables us to grow and be full of joy. Apostle Paul in 2 Corinthians chapter 12 verse 10 (NIV), put it simply but powerfully stated that "when I am weak, then I am strong." We must spend time in God's presence so that our heart or spirit through the power of the Holy Spirit can receive the peace of God, which transcends all understanding, will guard your hearts and your minds in Christ Jesus, so that our joy may be full and having strength for day-to-day victories in the issues of life.

Our lives must be governed by the word of God and faith in His word that never fails, even in the event of contrary situations, the arms of Jesus are open wrap yourself around His unfailing love and everlasting peace and joy. God is faithful and merciful and will never leave us nor forsake us in the moment of our needs, He is always present feelings has nothing to do with it, but faith anchored in His unfailing word of truth. The spirit of fear is the spirit of failure, so resist and reject it. Devine deposit is present in your life, but you must discover your potential, strength and talents and focus your total power to use them to succeed in life. It is dangerous to focus on your weakness or failures, rather let them challenge you to bring out the overcomers in you, that is by bringing out the best in you. Past failures should challenge you to always strive to do better because you are like a tree planted by streams of water, the fruit of success eventually come if keep on it without giving up. We can do all this through him who gives me strength. We find our hope solid, and we see fulfilments of his promises along the way. Hope grows through our strong determination to continue to do or trying to chieve something, despite problems or trials and this produces perseverance in us. Hope in God builds in us through tribulation and enables us to know why we are who we are, and we know where we are going.

This all-important tried-character quality is one of the keys to develop a positive attitude through in-built rugged strong determination to succeed. This tried-character quality should be celebrated with gladness, rejoicing because it is an indication that you made to succeed, and you are not a person that gives up at the slightest problem. Believers are called overcomers, *i.e.,* perseveres. Tried character is a distinguishing trait of those walk in the Spirit. Challenges are steppingstone to make it through the valley to the other side or to move to the next level. Perseverance is done in a careful attitude when difficulties continue.

When multiple challenges confront us, perseverance will grow into hope if it is not stagnant. That means that we must anchor our thoughts in the Word of God, which says "Not by might nor by power, but by my Spirit,' says the Lord Almighty" Zechariah 4:6 (NIV). These are strong hope-producing power, to overcome challenges. We are called to endurance and not being passive, but to have strong back-bone to fight back to step our foot on and repossess our promise land. It is that combination of enduring backed-up with faith in God's Word that produces hope. Romans 15:13 (NIV) "May the God of hope fill you with all joy and peace as you trust in him, so that you may overflow with hope by the power of the Holy Spirit." My friends always remember that through perseverance and the encouragement of the Scriptures we might have hope. The word of encouragement for us is always to persevere, no matter what the situation.

The scripture in James chapter 1 verse 12 (NIV) says, "Blessed is the one who perseveres under trial because, having stood the test, that person will receive the crown of life that the Lord has promised to those who love him." Perseverance reveals our trust and belong to the Almighty, if we keep looking to Jesus as the author and finisher of our faith, no matter how many times we fail, or how discouraged we have become due to multiple challenges, because we know whom we have believed, and we are persuaded that God is able to keep that which we have committed unto Him against that Day. Therefore, we are not ashamed, because we know in whom we have put our trust.

Challenges in life journey are the necessary training school of endurance to develop steadfastness, an essential quality that strengthens our character, which builds our confidence that we are victorious in Christ Jesus and God will see us through any obstacles on our way and empowered us to move forward. The power of perseverance to overcome difficulties and steadfastness is a true indication of our strong faith through the blueprints of authentic hope. The will power and the experience God's favour and love through the Spirit comforts us as we go through tribulations and strengthen us to move beyond the roadblocks. Endurance in the heart of any person comes through confronting and overcoming trials.

Success in life come from "perseverance", "endurance", "patience", "fortitude", "steadfastness", the capacity to hold out or bear up in the face of difficulty. The journey of life calls for determination when things are not going the proper direction, however we rejoice in the hope of the glory of God. Not only so, but we also rejoice in our sufferings, because we know that suffering produces perseverance; perseverance, character; and character, hope. And hope does not disappoint us, because God has poured out his love into our hearts by the Holy Spirit, whom he has given us. God uses trials to prepare us for His purposes and to prove Himself powerful and reliable. This is the classroom to develop hope, perseverance, patience, and matured character.

The Scripture in the book of James reveals that we must trust the Lord and keep our eyes our eyes on Him because God have purpose in trials and also give wisdom for His glory. That is one of the reasons we must ask for wisdom in faith during trials, so that the Lord who is kind and merciful will respond to our requests so that we can acknowledge the good and the purpose in trials.

Finally, my friends stress is what strengthen our muscles, likewise we grow spiritually stronger if we faithfully endure. Our hope stagnates without difficulty. Without stress, our muscles are content with their current size and strength. Stress enables our muscles to be stronger and operates properly. The Lord wants us to trust Him in the trials of life, in order to use the difficult trial to build-up our character or personality. The Lord permits us to go through trials to test, prove, and strengthen our faith in Him. Perseverance in difficult trial will mature us and will make Christians to be more like Jesus Christ our Saviour.

# *Peace*

The scripture says 2 Thessalonians chapter 3 verse 16 (NIV) says "Now may the Lord of peace himself give you peace at all times and in every way. The Lord be with all of you." Thank God for John chapter 14 verse 27 (NIV), Jesus has given us his peace "Peace I leave with you; my peace I give you. I do not give to you as the world gives. Do not let your hearts be troubled and do not be afraid." Therefore, it is our responsibility to keep this peace in our heart. Isaiah chapter 26 verse 3 (NIV) "You will keep in perfect peace those whose minds are steadfast, because they trust in you."

Peace is a state of quietness of spirit that transcends circumstances. In the scripture peace is as a gift from God. God is peace, then to know God is to live and walk in His peace. The closer we draw to Jesus, the more we can enjoy this peace. In John chapter 14 verse 27 (NIV), Jesus said, "Peace I leave with you; my peace I give you. I do not give to you as the world gives. Do not let your hearts be troubled and do not be afraid." So, whatever is the situation, peace is found in the presence of Jesus. We draw close to God for us to experience His peace and we come to the throne of grace and into the presence of the Lord through our Lord Jesus, sacrificial birth, death, ascension, and resurrection. Jesus came so that we can have life and have it more abundantly. Therefore, having been justified by faith, we have peace with God through our Lord Jesus Christ.

Peace of mind is a state of concord or tranquillity. God will keep us in perfect peace when our minds are steadfast on Jesus, through the Word of God in our heart because our trust Him. We are created to have inner calm, whatever the situation or circumstances that is going on within, outside and around us. The scriptures Philippians chapter 4 verses 11 to 13 (NIV) says, "I am not saying this because I am in need, for I have learned to be content whatever the circumstances. I know what it is to be in need, and I know what it is to have plenty. I have learned the secret of being content in any and every situation, whether well fed or hungry, whether living in plenty or in want. I can do all this through him who gives me strength."

Peace of mind allows us to be calm, strong, and confident in themselves and our God given abilities which enables to continue learn, grow, do, and develop into the person God has created us to be. My friends, do you know that the peace of God is present even in the mist of challenges, struggles, trials, difficulties, worries, and fear. Yes, that is correct because God does not only promise to give us peace, but He has actually given us peace that passes all understanding, and desires to keep us in perfect peace. We must choose to stay in the presence of God, irrespective of the pressure of life. Grace and peace be yours in abundance through the knowledge of God and of Jesus our Lord.

God's divine power has given us everything we need for a godly life through our knowledge of him who called us by his own glory and goodness.

Although God has given us His very great and precious promises, so that through them we may participate in the divine nature, having escaped the corruption in the world caused by evil desires, must believe it, claim it, confess, or declare it and receive it by acting on it through faith. The life of the person filled with hope and trust that implicitly put their child like faith in the Lord, have joy, gladness, and peace that passes all understanding. When we take time to step back from the pressure of life and come into the presence of God, He can speak promises of hope and comfort over our circumstances.

Peace is found in the promises of hope and comfort over our circumstances. Our mind set must accept the fact that in the middle of difficulty lies opportunity, and meditation in the word of God is one of the ways to strengthen our right thinking and believe. The Lord will keep in perfect peace those whose minds are steadfast because they trust in Him. Trusting in the Lord and hoping in Him is being certain of the existence of things we cannot see. In trusting you can experience the peace of God when you come to Him in humility and accept the blessings, the Lord has planned and wants you to have through Jesus Christ.

There are times in the journey of life when you may feel overwhelmed and do not know what to do or the next decision or action to take, that very moment, when you need most to feed more on the word of God. A believer should avoid being anxious or worry about the issues of life but when you find yourself filled with anxiety and worry that should be an opportunity to spend more quiet time to confess the Scripture, listen to encouraging sermons and worship the Lord in prayers. We all need to be reminded of the strength and the peace God has for us, so that we can take them by faith and walk in the light.

Philippians chapter 4 verses 6 to 7 (NIV) says "Do not be anxious about anything, but in every situation, by prayer and petition, with thanksgiving, present your requests to God. And the peace of God, which transcends all understanding, will guard your hearts and your minds in Christ Jesus." We are commanded not be anxious about anything, but in every situation, by prayer and petition, with thanksgiving, present our requests to God. So that the peace of God, which transcends all understanding, will guard our hearts and minds in Christ Jesus.

The desire for peace is one thing we all have in common, but most people do not know to have rest or a peace of mind. Some are not really sure that God's love desires that everyone of us should have an abundant life, live to the fullest and that includes being at peace. Such peace can only be experienced in His presence, when we humble ourselves before the Lord Jesus by accepting the goodness and blessings, we have in Him. Blessed are those who through faith and hope possess the keys to walk in the grace and favor of God to receive the blessing and to participate in the prepaid goodies in the table of the Lord for those who trust Him in the presence of everyone.

Peace within comes from setting our mind on the finished work of Jesus Christ and maintaining our focus on His Grace. We must have a clear vision of our most important desires prioritized into a plan to achieve the set goals. A desired purpose to achieve specific goal during our time in this world. I love this verse in the book of Psalm chapter 119 verse 165 (NIV), "Great [Abundant] peace have those who love your law, and nothing can make them stumble."

## The fear Of Failure

The fear of failure is common to mankind. Anyone that has a big vision and desire to be successful knows that there is always a possibility of not achieving the set goals, but failure should never be an option, but a stimulus to be successful. Some fears are irrational while some are mostly due to lack of knowledge. There is the saying that "Imagination is more important than knowledge. Knowledge is limited, imagination encircles the world." However, limited knowledge could generate unnecessary fear. Such fear could paralyze great opportunities and promotes wasted talents and gifts. The imagination of fear is actually worse than the actual situation but unfortunately, the people under this bondage give in to the imagine fear and are open to defeat in that situation and some probably in life.

God will keep anyone in perfect peace, whose mind is stayed on Jesus, because he [or her] trusts in the Lord Jesus, who is the author and finisher of our faith, who will perfect that which concerns us. The Lord will fulfil His purpose for us; your love, O Lord, endures forever, do not abandon the works of your hands. The perfecting is of that which is according to God's will, which exactly is what concerns us more than anything else in this life. The word of God gives us security or assurance that God has committed himself to fulfilling his purposes in us. That should be our anchor to comfort, strengthen, empower, and encourage us knowing that as we are pursuing God's purposes, whatever the situation, circumstances or how things may seem or not seem to be, God has promised not to forsake us but will bring that work to perfect completion.

Every successful person has this anchor of faith to bring the work to perfect completion. However, the fact that we all have a certain fear of failing, has brought defeat to many people who could have done great things with their talents while those who courageously defeated the fear of failure are successful people in their various fields of talents. The common traits are that although they all had partial failures in various stages, but they tenaciously kept on it until they were successful. Failure could not stop them because despite many unsuccessful attempts they finally achieved their goals.

## Encourage One Another

As a matter of fact, it is awesome when someone believe in you and encourage you to use your talents to achieve your goals. The scripture in chapter 1 Thessalonians 5 verse 11 (NIV) says: "Therefore encourage (admonish, exhort) one another and build (strengthen and build up) each other up, just as in fact you are doing." We appreciate those who encourage us, and we are blessed by their words of encouragement because in encouraging others, we all develop and accomplish our dreams, so we should encourage others to maximize their potential. We are created to always encourage and influence in a positive way other who are going through challenges.

## Self-Belief or Self-Doubt

Our generosity and ability to appreciate the success of others has power to encourage and bless others in a way greater than we can imagine in our minds. There are celebrated cases where someone may not initially believe in him [her]self and someone came along with encouragement to diffuses these doubting of self or ability. This is great, but if nobody encourages you what happens? It is good to believe in yourself, before anyone can believe in you i.e., self-belief. Discouragement and lack of self-belief are two of the greatest hope or vision killers.

My friend, every time you get tempted to give up on your dream, meditate on what Davide did in 1 Samuel chapter 30 verse 6 (NIV), "David was greatly distressed because the men were talking of stoning him; each one was bitter in spirit because of his sons and daughters. But David found strength in the Lord his God." The scripture says that "David found strength in the Lord his God" (NIV), but in another version it says, "But David encouraged himself in the Lord" (KJV). Do you agree with me that, if David needed to encourage himself in the Lord or found strength in the Lord his God, so will you and me. And if he can do it, you and I can do it. Our self-talk in this situation should always be, "If David can do it, I can do it. The same God that was with Davide, is on my side and I will not quit but fight for my dream."

I can do all things through Christ who is my strength. When you are in distress or in moment of despair and you need encouragement and strength, look within you, the Comforter the Holy Spirit of God. He is able to do exceedingly and abundantly above all we can think or ask. We should practice encouraging ourselves in the Lord and speak the word of God to our situation. We must refuse to be discouraged, by acknowledging our help comes from the Lord who empowers us to get wealth and success. The time you feel like giving up, is the very moment to be strong in the Lord and in the power of His might.

The scripture in Romans chapter 15 verse 4 (NIV), says, "For everything that was written in the past was written to teach us, so that through the endurance taught in the Scriptures and the encouragement they provide we might have hope." If we all could believe more in our Individual abilities and use our given talents, mankind would advance greatly with more successful people at an incredible pace. We all have various opportunities irrespective of self-doubt, with courage and determination, we depart from our personal so-called comfort zones and push ourselves to achieve our desired dreams.

However, if we compare ourselves unfavourably to others, it destroys our self-esteem, confident and determination which leads eventually to decreases enormously our self-belief, when we believe other people are better, know better, or could do better than us. We must resist from comparing our situation with to others and focus on our dreams and goals, most especially on our own path to achieve success. When we lose our focus by allowing too much influence from outside, we lose not only our way and the war in the mind and eventually our chance for peace of mind. The scripture says, in Colossian chapter 3 verse 15 (NIV), "Let the peace of Christ rule in your hearts, since as members of one body you were called to peace. And be thankful."

The plan of God for us has always been that we have victory over challenges, having abundance and live-in perfect peace. God does not want us to live in worry, fear, doubt, and unbelief. God wants us to be healthy and have a sound mind. As a matter of truth, worry is a sin designed by Satan to keep our mind and heart on the problems instead of looking unto Jesus the author and finisher of our faith. Deuteronomy chapter 32 verse 11 (NIV), says, "like an eagle that stirs up its nest and hovers over its young, that spreads its wings to catch them and carries them aloft." This peace of God that surpasses understanding should govern the heart of every person.

This tranquillity of the heart in the mist of difficulties, trials, and challenges, is called unspeakable, because although you are confident because you have it, others cannot understand it and you cannot explain to them in words. God invites us to cast our cares upon Him and then let go of them, because there are some attitudes that can hinder our ability to receive the peace of God. When we decide to worry rather than trust God and the ability or talent given to us, we may lose our peace. Worry is the enemy of peace, because it is meditating on a bad vision for the future. We cannot live in peace when we panic and fear the unknown or future.

The word of God instructs us continuously not to worry and fear. It is one of those things the word of God directly commands us to not do, because worry is a sin. We are invited to trust God, because blessed is the person whose trust is the Lord almighty God. Trust means that whatever may happen, we have set our hearts to believe God. However, this trust does not mean we assume that God will give us whatever we want, because this could lead to disappointment and frustration, which eventually may steal our joy and peace.

Our anchor and trust are in the Lord Jesus because He is the source of this peace of mind. This peace will protect our heart and our thoughts in Christ Jesus, because in Him we find life, strength, and true rest, the scripture says, 1 Thessalonians chapter 5 verse 23 (NIV), says, "May God himself, the God of peace, sanctify you through and through. May your whole spirit, soul and body be kept blameless at the coming of our Lord Jesus Christ." Peace is not the absence of challenges or trials, but the presence of Jesus Christ. When we chose to Trust and submit to God, we can have this peace described as a tranquil state of faith and appreciation. This comes from our submission, humility, and courage to experience God's peace, looking unto God's wisdom more than our natural knowledge, understanding and abilities. Jesus is God's gift of peace, love, righteousness, light, and life. He is ever present grace, favor

and peace to us in all aspect of life. These gifts are given by God as the fruit of the human spirit. In Him we live and move. Acts chapter 17 verse 28 (NIV), says, "For in him we live and move and have our being. As some of your own poets have said, 'We are his offspring." Jesus is the same today, tomorrow and forever, therefore our relationship with the Jesus Christ we have the reassures of true security in life. Grace and peace be multiplied to you in every area of life. The scripture in 2 Peter chapter 1 verse 2 (NIV), says, "Grace and peace be yours in abundance through the knowledge of God and of Jesus our Lord."

Psalm chapter 119 verse 165 (NIV), "Great peace have those who love your law, and nothing can make them stumble."There is great blessing in the life of any person who set his [or her] mind to believe the word of God. It is the harmony and calmness of body, mind, and spirit that supersedes earthly circumstances. Come near to God and He will come near to you. A wonderful blessing of love and grace to mankind in agreement with God's character. which transcends all understanding," This peace of God lives independently of challenges, trials, and circumstances, which the world can neither give nor take away.

God wants us to live always in this kind of peace. The closer we are in our relationship to God, the more of this grace and peace we can experience in our life. The word of God encourages us to grow or increase in our relationship with Jesus Christ, trusting God to give us more and more grace and peace as we grow in our knowledge of God and Jesus our Lord. The initial peace that comes from having our consciences wiped clean grows as we get to know God better. We must allow the peace of Christ rule more and more in our hearts, because as members of one body we were called to peace. When we dwell constantly in the secret place in communion with God, we can remain peaceful, even in difficult situations and circumstances. God is always our refuge and my fortress and in Him we will trust.

## Living in Peace (Solid Rock)

Peace is that virtue and power that will enable you go through the storms of life. It is a foundation of power that makes life more meaningful, enjoyable, and fruitful.

In the book of Matthew chapter 7 verse 24 to 27 (NIV), Jesus says "Therefore everyone who hears these words of mine and puts them into practice is like a wise man who built his house on the rock. The rain came down, the streams rose, and the winds blew and beat against that house; yet it did not fall, because it had its foundation on the rock. But everyone who hears these words of mine and does not put them into practice is like a foolish man who built his house on sand. The rain came down, the streams rose, and the winds blew and beat against that house, and it fell with a great crash."

On the sermon "Build Your House on the Rock", Jesus commanded us to build our life on the word of faith. Romans chapter 10 verse 17 (NKJV), "So, then faith *comes* by hearing, and hearing by the Word of God." A house built on Jesus Christ the "Rock" is a house built on the foundation of the word of God. Therefore everyone who hears these Words of Faith and acts on them may be compared to a wise man who built his house on the rock and the rain fell and the floods came and the winds blew and slammed against the house and yet it did not fall for it hadn't been built and founded on the foundation of the Word of God, everyone who hears these Words of Faith and does not act on them will be like a foolish man who built his house on the sand the rains fell and the floods came and the winds blew and slammed against that house and it fell and great was its fall.

Peace comes by building your life on the foundation of the word of God. The Lord will keep anyone in perfect peace, whose mind is stayed on God almighty (through the Word): because such person trusted in God. Keep your trust in the Lord for ever: for in the Lord JEHOVAH is everlasting strength. Peace is tested in trials, difficulties, tribulations, and hardships. Our respond in these situations and circumstances determines the peace in our life. They reveal who we are and what we are like and what our foundation is built on. It determines our level or state of peace of mind.

We must build a firm foundation that will make it possible to withstand all the situations in the journey of life. A disciplined life to withstand the curves and storm of life, so that you do not get blown away when our foundation is tested. Peace to be victorious when the torrent of temptation comes your way and when the storm of trial comes your away in disappointment? How much peace do you respond to partial defeats, difficulties, and the travails of life? Do you respond in perfect peace to criticisms and trials? Does failures and challenges build your muscles? When the faced with rejection and obstacles come instead of maintaining your peace and finding strength are you weaken? Does challenges and failure build you stronger? In times of trials do you have enough courage and strength to move forward with your goals?

You will only discover how strong you are when you know and acknowledge your weaknesses? If you do not know what your weaknesses are, you will never know your strength, capabilities, and potentials. The strong faith of Abraham was discovered in an obedience demonstrated by his peace of mind when tested by God to sacrifice his only son. In Genesis chapter 22 verse 7 to 8 (NIV), Isaac spoke up and said to his father Abraham, Father? Yes, my son? Abraham replied. The fire and wood are here, Isaac said, but where is the lamb for the burnt offering? Abraham answered, God himself will provide the lamb for the burnt offering, my son." And the two of them went on together."

## The Story "Abraham Tested" - Genesis chapter 22 verse 1 through 19 (NIV)

*Sometime later God tested Abraham. He said to him, "Abraham! Here I am," he replied. Then God said, "Take your son, your only son, whom you love—Isaac—and go to the region of Moriah. Sacrifice him there as a burnt offering on a mountain I will show you. Early the next morning Abraham got up and loaded his donkey. He took with him two of his servants and his son Isaac. When he had cut enough wood for the burnt offering, he set out for the place God had told him about. On the third day Abraham looked up and saw the place in the distance. He said to his servants, Stay here with the donkey while I and the boy go over there. We will worship and then we will come back to you. Abraham took the wood for the burnt offering and placed it on his son Isaac, and he himself carried the fire and the knife. As the two of them went on together, Isaac spoke up and said to his father Abraham, "Father? "Yes, my son?" Abraham replied. "The fire and wood are here," Isaac said, "but where is the lamb for the burnt offering? Abraham answered, "God himself will provide the lamb for the burnt offering, my son." And the two of them went on together. When they reached the place, God had told him about, Abraham built an altar there and arranged the wood on it. He bound his son Isaac and laid him on the altar, on top of the wood. Then he reached out his hand and took the knife to slay his son. But the angel of the LORD called out to him from heaven, "Abraham! Abraham!" "Here I am," he replied. "Do not lay a hand on the boy," he said. "Do not do anything to him. Now I know that you fear God, because you have not withheld from me your son, your only son." Abraham looked up and there in a thicket he saw a ram[a] caught by its horns. He went over and took the ram and sacrificed it as a burnt offering instead of his son. So, Abraham called that place The Lord will Provide. And to this day it is said, On the mountain of the Lord it will be provided. The angel of the LORD called to Abraham from heaven a second time and said, I swear by myself, declares the Lord, that because you have done this and have not withheld your son, your only son, I will surely bless you and make your descendants as numerous as the stars in the sky and as the sand on the seashore. Your descendants will take possession of the cities of their enemies, and through your offspring all nations on earth will be blessed, because you have obeyed me.* Then Abraham returned to his servants, and they set off together for Beersheba. And Abraham stayed in Beersheba.

# *Below Let us Deal with Some of the Things that could Seriously Affect your Peace.*

- **Practise Forgiveness (Mistakes, Hurts and Offence)**
- **Exchange your Unforgiveness for Peace**
- **Meditation**
- **Unclutter your Mind and Life!**
- **Be Honest with Yourself**
- **Focus on Goals you can Change.**
- **Gratitude (Be Grateful Always)**
- **Be Generous**
  - o **Example Of Great Generosity in the Old-Testament**
  - o **Example Of Great Generosity in the New-Testament**
- **Fight The Good Fight of Faith (Endurance)**
- **Boundaries and Limits on Yourself Means Growth**
- **Do not let your Past Failure Defines You**
- **Learn From Past Experiences**
- **Learn To Deal with Failures**
- **Do not Let Other People's Negative Criticism Define You**
- **Find a balance in your Life.**
- **Rejection and Denial is Common**
- **Accept and let it Go!**
- **Ask and Wait for the Season**
- **Fear Not**
- **Cultivate Good Habits or Routines**
- **Be strong in the Lord and in the power of His Might**
- **Rejoice Always**

### Practise Forgiveness (Mistakes, Hurts and Offence)

The scripture in Ephesians chapter 4 verse 32 (NIV), commands all Christians to "Be kind and compassionate to one another, forgiving each other, just as in Christ God forgave you." It is, therefore, absolutely important for everyone to know what forgiveness is as well as what it is not. Unforgiveness is the breeding ground for more evil forces or spirits like bitterness, resentment, unkindness, and anger. It separates the believer from enjoying the benefits of dependence on the wisdom of God and most especially it separates him [or her] from growing more of the Fruit of the Spirit in their lives. Therefore, it is the easiest access, route or doorway to Satan claiming or occupying territory in the lives of Christians.

The Revelation chapter 1 verse 4 (NIV), says." To the seven churches in the province of Asia: Grace and peace to you from him who is, and who was, and who is to come, and from the seven spirits[a] before his throne." The Lord provides healing and blessing through forgiveness, but unforgiving spirit a person from fellowship peacefully with God. They actually consume and control the mind of the person, so such a person cannot have a sound mind. It certainly prevents a person from having the mind of Christ. The sad thing is that the longer this grudge is carrying over, the more they gain control the thoughts, feelings, and actions of the person. It eventually steals the freedom and liberty of the person because the spend most of their time thinking about the offence or hurt.

### Exchange your Unforgiveness for Peace

Forgiveness is a decision that comes from the will of a person. Unless a person takes a decision to forgive an offence, if he [she] decides to hold on to it, instead of forgiven by faith and being set free, the person's mind gets hooked on recycle trying to resolve something that only the love and grace of God can solve properly. The ultimate result of unhealthy focusing and re-visiting thoughts of these past painful events is melancholy and depression.

It is a steals peace trying to control or re-live a past hurt, an unfair treatment, hopelessness for justice or injustice, denied right, and mistreatment that happened in the past. There is no hope, joy, and most especially peace of mind in any act of hatred, holding grudges, vengeance, revenge, and bitterness. Forgives is the mother of hope and hope can only take root in the soil of "allowing to let go by faith in the finished work of Jesus Christ the unhealthy past events." It is not humanly possible for anyone to right a wrong that has occurred in the past. Peace in forgiveness is possible only through the anchor by faith on the finished work of Jesus Christ. My friends, as He is so we in this world, so let us be imitators of our Lord Jesus Christ, and the peace of God, which transcends all understanding, will guard your hearts and your minds in Christ Jesus.

## Meditation

Meditation in the word of God bring understanding and truth into the heart of mankind. It impacts the revelation truth and the revelation knowledge to enable the person to walk according to the light of the word of faith. Psalm 119 verse 15 (ESV) says, I will meditate on your precepts and fix my eyes on your ways." Meditation give access for God to get actively involved with the life of mankind, because the person gets overtaken by the blessing of God.

There is peace in meditation based on the word of God. Psalm chapter 19 verse 14 (ESV) says, "Let the words of my mouth and the meditation of my heart be acceptable in your sight, O Lord, my rock, and my redeemer." This puts the human spirit in conscious contact with God. It gives peace and quiet against the stresses of life and in hard times reminding us of all the various great powerful promises in the word of God, that offer peace to the troubled heart.

God almighty is the originator of meditation, so it is very essential that you spend time every day in meditating in the word of the Lord. In the book of Joshua chapter 1 verse 8 (NIV), God said to Joshua, "Keep this Book of the Law always on your lips; meditate on it day and night, so that you may be careful to do everything written in it. Then you will be prosperous and successful." The knowledge of the truth that God's love is renewed every morning, it gives us great hope in the battles of life that steals joy and most especially peace. The Psalmist says in Psalm chapter 119 verse 98 to 113 (NIV), "Your commands are always with me and make me wiser than my enemies. I have more insight than all my teachers, for I meditate on your statutes. I have more understanding than the elders, for I obey your precepts. I have kept my feet from every evil path so that I might obey your word. I have not departed from your laws, for you yourself have taught me. How sweet are your words to my taste, sweeter than honey to my mouth! I gain understanding from your precepts; therefore, I hate every wrong path."

Mediating in the word of God is like rays of light breaking through the darkest night because God's steadfast love never ceases; his mercies never come to an end; they are new every morning, great is your faithfulness. Human inconsistency, fragility, and changes in time and season does not change the love of God, which is in Christ Jesus.

## Unclutter your Mind and Life!

We must decide to set our mind clean from cabbages by meditating day and night and keeping God's promises on our mouth. Trust in the Lord with all your heart, and do not lean on your own understanding because whoever trusts in his own mind is not wise, but he who walks in wisdom will be delivered, God shall provide direction to the person according to His wisdom by the power of the Holy Spirit. We must also give careful attendance to do everything written in the Holy Scriptures., The word of God, clearly states that if we do these things then we will be prosperous and successful. These instructions were the direction the Lord strongly commanded Joshua.

The reason many believers have cabbages in their minds is because they engage within internal dialogue with the devil. The devil gate crash into their minds without any authority to plant seeds of doubt, fear with questions. Some of the self-talk questions of "why" and "why me" are probably suggestions from the dark forces. Meditate on the word and learn to ignore satanic questions or to answer the devil with "it is written," or else you may lose your control.

The devil will ask you series of questions tricking your mind to accept and believe they are yours and then give you satanic false answers to back them up. As God commanded Joshua, we must decide to set our mind to keep the promises of God always on our lips; meditate on it day and night and be careful to do everything written in it, then you will be prosperous and successful. The scripture gives us a clear example of the commands the almighty God gave to Joshua at that critical moment in his life and the lives of the people of Israel that enabled him to achieve the purpose of God for the people and his life.

## Be Honest with Yourself

Be honest with yourself and know your strength and weakness. Then focus on your strength, by so doing you are actually taking control of situation of your life. Every person has Devine deposit present in their life, but this must be discovered. The discovery of this potential, and talents is your responsibility, because there lies your strength. Discover your talents and set your mind to focus your total power to use them to succeed in life. It is unfortunate that most people are quick to identify their weakness and sadly they focus on what is wrong things, like the talents they lack, difficulties and unfavourable circumstances.

It is dangerous to focus on your weakness or failures, rather you should let them challenge you to bring out the overcomers in you, that is by bringing out the best in you. Fear if failure or past failures should challenge you to always strive to do better because you are like the man in the scripture, who is like a tree planted by streams of water, the fruit of success eventually will come if you keep on it without giving up.

Psalm chapter 1 verse 1 to 3 (NIV), says "Blessed is the one who does not walk in step with the wicked or stand in the way that sinners take or sit in the company of mockers, but whose delight is in the law of the Lord, and who meditates on his law day and night. That person is like a tree planted by streams of water, which yields its fruit in season and whose leaf does not wither - whatever they do prospers."

## Focus on Goals you can Change

Learn to focus on the situations you can change instead of wasting energy and precious time on what you cannot change. We can focus our hope on our dreams and goals, as we appreciate and rejoice in the present blessings. We must trust God who is forever omnipresent, omniscient, omnipotent, an ever-present help in time of trouble. God is our refuge and strength, an ever-present help in trouble.

Our trust, hope and focus should be anchored on the promises found in the words of the Lord. I utterly agree that the secret to being content in any situation, "to get the calm, the tranquillity, the peace" is to love God supremely.

## Gratitude (Be Grateful Always)

Be grateful always and express gratitude appreciating the goodness in life. Psalm chapter 118 verse 24 (NIV), says "The Lord has done it this very day; let us rejoice today and be glad." Gratitude is a spontaneous feeling of making conscious efforts to appreciate and count one's blessings. 1 Thessalonians chapter 5 verse 18 (NIV), says "give thanks in all circumstances; for this is God's will for you in Christ Jesus." There are a lot of benefits being grateful. The rewards for gratitude are enormous and could be both social and personal. People feel grateful for family, relatives, relationship, colleague, and institutions. Colossians chapter 3 verse 17 (NIV), says "And whatever you do, whether in word or deed, do it all in the name of the Lord Jesus, giving thanks to God the Father through him."

Ephesians chapter 2 verse 16 (NIV), says "and in one body to reconcile both of them to God through the cross, by which he put to death their hostility." The emotional positive climate that comes from gratitude goes very deep down to soul of mankind and flows outwardly. It is an emotion that makes a person feel happier or more joyful. Acts chapter 24 verse 3 (NIV), says "Everywhere and in every way, most excellent Felix, we acknowledge this with profound gratitude." Gratitude could be an attitude or a part of someone's personality. Some people find it easy and even feel joyful being grateful at all times. Psalm chapter 9 verse 1 (NIV), says "I will give thanks to you, Lord, with all my heart; I will tell of all your wonderful deeds." In fact, it is part of their habit to express always with gladness their gratitude. These are cheerful and joyful people who appreciate every good thing in life.

Being grateful is an acknowledgement of the goodness of the heart. It shows a positive or optimistic outlook. There are challenges, trials, and difficulties but it is a decision to focus on good thing in life, that is done by acknowledging the benefits and blessing, we have or given to us. Psalm 103 verses 1 to 2 (NIV), says "raise the Lord, my soul; all my inmost being, praise his holy name. Praise the Lord, my soul, and forget not all his benefits -." Life is not perfect, and we are not perfect, however a positive outlook at life, the scripture encourages us to remember the benefits which are the goodness things in our life. The scripture says in Philemon's Love and Faith that the sharing of your faith may become effective by the acknowledgment of every good thing which is in you in Christ Jesus.

Philemon chapter 1 verse 4 to 6 (NIV), says "I always thank my God as I remember you in my prayers, because I hear about your love for all his holy people and your faith in the Lord Jesus. I pray that your partnership with us in the faith may be effective in deepening your understanding of every good thing we share for the sake of Christ." We acknowledge that this goodness or benefit is God sending divine helpers to us. These dependence on other people or institutions are our resources but our source is the almighty God. We acknowledge with appreciation the help we receive from God through people or institutions, to accomplish the goodness and benefits in our lives. Our faith becomes effective by the acknowledgment of every good thing which is in us in Christ Jesus.

Gratitude should be a lifestyle and not something to try for some days. It should be a deep decision taken to be grateful in life and showing appreciation to everyone that has supported you along the journey. Every Christian should be grateful to the Father, the son and the Holy Spirit for life and appreciate or be grateful for the people God have put in your life. Be grateful for an accomplishment, blessings in a difficult situation, a recent lesson learnt. Celebrate every little success, always find some positive to celebrate about your journey of life. There is one good thing to celebrate if we look deeper, so find something good in the mist of difficulties to focus on and celebrate.

Learn to be grateful for an accomplishment you are proud about and share with others with joy. an Create a list of things and opportunities you had and be grateful for them. There could be in the list something you never thought you could achieve, there lies your hidden blessing in a difficult situation. Is there anything in this situation where you found comfort in the mist of trials and difficulties, this should be an opportunity for gratitude. Whatever circumstances you have gone through in life, any lesson learnt from this situation should become our source of gratitude, because we also gain experience from past pains.

## Be Generous

The scripture in 1 Timothy 6 verses 17 through 19 (NIV), says "Command those who are rich in this present world not to be arrogant nor to put their hope in wealth, which is so uncertain, but to put their hope in God, who richly provides us with everything for our enjoyment. Command them to do good, to be rich in good deeds, and to be generous and willing to share. In this way they will lay up treasure for themselves as a firm foundation for the coming age, so that they may take hold of the life that is truly life." Giving is more important than wanting more than what one needs. In 2 Corinthians chapter 9 verse 11 (NIV), says "You will be enriched in every way so that you can be generous on every occasion, and through us your generosity will result in thanksgiving to God."

What does the Bible say about generosity? There are many biblical verses that encourage us to be generous and kind with others as our generosity will be returned to us by God. Proverbs 11:24 (NIV), states "One person gives freely, yet gains even more; another withholds unduly, but comes to poverty." It is righteous to practice generosity with our family, friends, and community, because we gain favor with God by being charitable voluntarily, and we also produce goodwill among our fellow humans. When we are generous in our giving to other people or institutions, God returns the same measure of generosity to us: The word in Luke chapter 6 verse 38 (NIV), says "Give, and it will be given to you. A good measure, pressed down, shaken together, and running over, will be poured into your lap. For with the measure you use, it will be measured to you."

Our attitude is important in seed planting, so we should not despise the size of our offering, what we have is given in faith. Genesis chapter 8 verse 22 (NIV), says "As long as the earth endures, seedtime and harvest, cold and heat, summer and winter, day and night." It is better when we step out in faith and give and also it is not a good practice to procrastinate or postpone our given until we have an increase or special bonus. The good news is that something is activated when we give with a gratitude heart. Giving generosity is always rewarded. Proverbs chapter 18 verse 16 (NIV), says

"A gift opens the way and ushers the giver into the presence of the great." God loves a cheerful giver because it is a demonstration of our gratitude. Each one must give as he has decided in his heart, not reluctantly or under compulsion, for God loves a cheerful giver. We are encouraged to avoid giving grudgingly or complain or murmur after given because this is a sign of an underlying heart condition. God loves a cheerful giver because our offerings must come from a glad or joyful heart.

In Exodus chapter 35 verse 22 (NIV), says "All who were willing, men and women alike, came and brought gold jewellery of all kinds: brooches, earrings, rings and ornaments. They all presented their gold as a wave offering to the Lord." Our giving should come from the heart and must be voluntary and should be a product of cheerful attitude. This voluntary and cheerful giving will always be rewarded by God who loves, and blesses a cheerful giver, as it written in book of Proverbs chapter 22 verse 9 (NIV), "The generous will themselves be blessed, for they share their food with the poor." Our God loves to bless us exceedingly and abundantly with goodness and prosperity, and loves us to be generous like Jesus, because giving cheerfully is the grace of God demonstrated through us. So, giving to other people is like giving to God and generosity is always fevered. Proverbs chapter 11 verse 24 through 25 (NIV), says "One person gives freely, yet gains even more; another withholds unduly, but comes to poverty. A generous person will prosper; whoever refreshes others will be refreshed." It is God using us as ambassadors of Christ to be a blessing, the word of God, encourages us to do good, to be rich in good works, to be generous and ready to share.

The fruit of generosity makes a person give selflessly to help those who are in need. Proverbs chapter 19 verse 17 (NIV), says "Whoever is kind to the poor lends to the Lord and he will reward them for what they have done." In fact, God blesses us to be a blessing or to be generous to other people, most especially to those in need and for the spread of the gospel. So, giving to other people does not just benefit the recipient, but the giver as well. Genesis chapter 14 verse 19 through 20 (NIV), says "and he blessed Abram, saying, Blessed be Abram by God Most High, Creator of heaven and earth. And praise be to God Most High, who delivered your enemies into your hand." Then Abram gave him a tenth of everything." The point is this: whoever sows sparingly will also reap sparingly, and whoever sows bountifully will also reap bountifully. Each one must give as he has decided in his heart, not reluctantly or under compulsion, for God loves a cheerful giver. And God is able to make all grace abound to you, so that having all sufficiency in all things at all times, you may abound in every good work.

Giving leads to more blessings in life. Proverbs chapter 21 verse 26 (NIV), says "All day long he craves for more, but the righteous give without sparing." Although some people do not believe in seed planting, that does not hinder the word of God, it actually hinders those who do not believe because according to your faith so shall it be to you. In 2 Corinthians chapter 8 verse 2 (NIV), says "In the midst of a very severe trial, their overflowing joy and their extreme poverty welled up in rich generosity." If you have a desire in your heart to have more of a particular thing, you plant seeds, even if it seems that is all you have, do not eat your seed simply plant it on good soil and watch God move on your behalf for a reward. We must learn to give, and it will be given to us. A good measure, pressed down, shaken together, and running over, will be poured into our lap. For with the measure we use, it will be measured to us.

That is why we must absolutely avoid complaining or boasting about our helping or giving things to other people or institutions, because we rob ourselves of a blessing from God and a chance to receive back from him. The encouragement is that generosity has great rewards, because the more you give i.e., if you plant seeds by faith on good soil, it will surely bring good harvest. Every Biblical principle, requires faith, because the just shall live by faith and that is exactly where God likes to work. He who supplies seed to the Sower and bread for food will supply and multiply your seed for sowing and increase the harvest of your righteousness. However, it is especially important explaining clearly that everyone should give what they can and want. "Each of you should give what you have decided in your heart to give, not reluctantly or under compulsion, for God loves a cheerful giver. And God is able to bless you abundantly, so that in all things at all times, having all that you need, you will abound in every good work." 2 Corinthians chapter 9 verses 7 to 8 (NIV)

## Example Of Great Generosity in the Old-Testament

The Bible is full of many examples of great generosity demonstrated men and women. Deuteronomy chapter 15 verse 7 to 8 (NIV), commands "If anyone is poor among your fellow Israelites in any of the towns of the land the LORD your God is giving you, do not be hard-hearted or tight-fisted toward them. Rather, be openhanded and freely lend them whatever they need." God give blessings to us and as such, people should give back to God to say thank you. In 2 Chronicles chapter 31 verse 12 (NIV), says "Then they faithfully brought in the contributions, tithes and dedicated gifts. Konaniah, a Levite, was the overseer in charge of these things, and his brother Shimei was next in rank."

In Exodus chapter 36 verse 1 through 7 (NIV), says "So Bezalel, Oholiab and every skilled person to whom the LORD has given skill and ability to know how to carry out all the work of constructing the sanctuary are to do the work just as the LORD has commanded. Then Moses summoned Bezalel and Oholiab and every skilled person to whom the LORD had given ability and who was willing to come and do the work. They received from Moses all the offerings the Israelites had brought to carry out the work of constructing the sanctuary. And the people continued to bring freewill offerings morning after morning. So, all the skilled workers who were doing all the work on the sanctuary left what they were doing and said to Moses, The people are bringing more than enough for doing the work the LORD commanded to be done. Then Moses gave an order, and they sent this word throughout the camp: No man or woman is to make anything else as an offering for the sanctuary. And so, the people were restrained from bringing more, because what they already had was more than enough to do all the work."

In the above passage the people continued to bring freewill offerings morning after morning. So, all the skilled craftsmen who were doing all the work on the sanctuary left their work and said to Moses, "The people are bringing more than enough for doing the work the Lord commanded to be done." Then Moses gave an order..." No man or woman is to make anything else as an offering for the sanctuary." And so, the people were restrained from bringing more.

God is happy when we share what we have like personal wealth, materials with people, most especially those we do not know or cannot give back to us. We trust God believing our seeds will mature and we shall reap bountiful harvest that are exceedingly abundantly above all that we ask or think. We keep planting seeds on good soil with faith and expecting to receive from God who is our source our abundance.

## Example Of Great Generosity in the New-Testament

In the Acts of the Apostles are well known examples for the sharing demonstrated among the believers. They devoted themselves to the apostles' teaching and fellowship, to the breaking of bread and the prayers. Due to this an awe came upon every soul, and many wonders and signs were being done through the apostles. All the people who believed were together and had all things in common. And they were selling their possessions and belongings and distributing the proceeds to all, as any had need.

The generosity in the below passages in Acts 2 and 4 was voluntary. It was not mandatory because the people did not have to sell their possessions and was not requested by the church to take such action. It must be crystal clear that it was not, and it is still not a prerequisite to be a Christian. The believers simply did it by their own free will.

In Acts chapter 2 verse 42 through 45 (NIV), says "They devoted themselves to the apostles' teaching and to fellowship, to the breaking of bread and to prayer. Everyone was filled with awe at the many wonders and signs performed by the apostles. All the believers were together and had everything in common. They sold property and possessions to give to anyone who had need."

In Acts chapter 4 verse 32 through 35 (NIV), says "All the believers were one in heart and mind. No one claimed that any of their possessions was their own, but they shared everything they had. With great power the apostles continued to testify to the resurrection of the Lord Jesus. And God's grace was so powerfully at work in them all that there were no needy persons among them. For from time to time those who owned land or houses sold them, brought the money from the sales, and put it at the apostles' feet, and it was distributed to anyone who had need."

## Fight The Good Fight of Faith (Endurance)

"You then, my son, be strong in the grace that is in Christ Jesus. And the things you have heard me say in the presence of many witnesses entrust to reliable people who will also be qualified to teach others. Join with me in suffering, like a good soldier of Christ Jesus. No one serving as a soldier gets entangled in civilian affairs, but rather tries to please his commanding officer. Similarly, anyone who competes as an athlete does not receive the victor's crown except by competing according to the rules. The hardworking farmer should be the first to receive a share of the crops. Reflect on what I am saying, for the Lord will give you insight into all this."

This is the instruction given to Timothy by Apostle Paul in 2 Timothy chapter 2 verse 1 through 7 (NIV). An appeal renewed not to give up or give in but to be like a soldier. The war is in the mind and peace comes from endurance by faith in the word of God. We must learn in mist of challenges to "endure" and "to persevere" with patient. The journey is marked with pain. We could miss out on God's direction and best for us if we fail to endure. Our endurance and perseverance have great rewards if we do not give up or give in to the pressure of trials. They have great value because the almighty is working to build us up into person of great significance and to bring out the best in us.

Sometimes we are impatient because we are not willing to endure any form of hardship and the cost is unachieved goals and lack of peace. The harvest in our hurt will only have meaning if we endure by going on without "throwing in the towel". In whatever situation there is always a harvest: "peaceful success for endurance" and "regretful failure for lack of endurance".

## Boundaries and Limits on Yourself Means Growth

Setting self-boundaries are natural and spiritual. In life, boundaries and limits are essential for indicating ownership of responsibility. The importance of ownership in our relationship cannot be over emphasized. Boundaries in a relationship is not fault finding in the other person, but helps me to identify ownership of feelings, attitudes, and behaviours. Jesus has set me free from condemnation and passing wrong judgement on other people. Jesus is made unto wisdom. 1 Corinthians chapter 1 verse 30 (NIV), says "It is because of him that you are in Christ Jesus, who has become for us wisdom from God - that is, our righteousness, holiness and redemption"

I have the wisdom of God in me to judge correctly, to whom the problem belongs, in the event of an issue. That means my relationship with another person requires, that I have a sense of ownership of myself and any attempt to control the life of another person is harmful to the relationship. That simply said, I cannot blame other people for my own behaviour, I must take responsibility or ownership for my own actions and behaviour.

Hebrews chapter 12 verse 14 (NIV), says "Make every effort to live in peace with everyone and to be holy; without holiness no one will see the Lord." This makes setting boundaries with me enjoyable and a source of peace. There is joy and a rest, because I stop struggling to defend myself, because peacefully I decline from putting blames on others and admit ownership of the problem. This action empowers me to take actions, to seek solutions and make the necessary changes to solve the problem.

The scripture says, in Mathew chapter 7 verse 3 through 5 (NIV), says "Why do you look at the speck of sawdust in your brother's eye and pay no attention to the plank in your own eye? How can you say to your brother, 'Let me take the speck out of your eye,' when all the time there is a plank in your own eye? You hypocrite, first take the plank out of your own eye, and then you will see clearly to remove the speck from your brother's eye."

I believe every person for the sake of peace and tranquillity, should set a couple of limits on himself [or herself]. This is important because boundaries in relationship is not the same as boundaries on other people but providing a platform for growth and personal development. It is the common ground for reconciliation and peace. Reconciliation is the restoration of friendly relations. In the

Scriptures, reconciliation involves a change in the relationship between God and man [or mankind and mankind]. There could have occurred a certain breakdown in the relationship, but now there has been a change from a state of enmity and fragmentation to one of fellowship, harmony, and peace.

That means that the first boundaries I set in a relationship, are with myself. This could be simply to deny myself certain freedoms to say or do whatever I would like, so as to attain a higher purpose. 2 Corinthians chapter 5 verses 18 and 19 (NIV), says "All this is from God, who reconciled us to himself through Christ and gave us the ministry of reconciliation: that God was reconciling the world to himself in Christ, not counting people's sins against them. And he has committed to us the message of reconciliation." This is the God kind of love, who took the first initiative, action to send our Lord and Saviour Jesus Christ to die, and to reconcile us from a problem of sin, our lost state which we have caused because of our sin nature.

Colossian chapter 3 verse 13 (NIV), "Bear with each other and forgive one another if any of you has a grievance against someone. Forgive as the Lord forgave you." Most cases, it practically useless and complete waste of time and energy our blaming others, because it does not often resolve the issue. Although we may share no blame in creating the problem, the most essential thing is the necessity to take immediate action or initiative to solve it. Mathew chapter 5 verse 9 (NIV), says "Blessed are the peacemakers, for they will be called children of God." God wants us to peace makers and desire that no matter who causes a problem, we are to take steps to solve it.

In Matthew chapter 18 verse 15 (NIV), the scriptures go on to say, "If your brother or sister sins, go and point out their fault, just between the two of you. If they listen to you, you have won them over." My friends, self-boundaries in any relationship enables me to take a deep look primarily at my own limitations, then with clarity and wisdom, take steps to confront peacefully those issues that need limits affecting others. This must be done properly, because any wrong decision could limit my own spiritual growth,

However, although we could be firm to communicate effectively what we will and what we will not tolerate, until other people respect our decision, but must not allow kindness and love to depart from us. Let everything be done in the spirit of respect, kindness, and love. We should always remember that our words are enormously powerful, but actions speaks louder than words, therefore we consider attentively the impact of our actions. Whatever we say or do we must work strive for things that bring joy. Love and peace, creating a better balance relationship-life.

## Do not let your Past Failure Defines You

Philippians chapter 3 verse 12 through 14 (NIV), "Not that I have already obtained all this, or have already arrived at my goal, but I press on to take hold of that for which Christ Jesus took hold of me. Brothers and sisters, I do not consider myself yet to have taken hold of it. But one thing I do: Forgetting what is behind and straining toward what is ahead, I press on toward the goal to win the prize for which God has called me heavenward in Christ Jesus."

But one thing I do: Forgetting what is behind and straining toward what is ahead, I press on toward the goal. We must take our eyes out of our past mistakes so that it does not become our defining features. The war in our mind must be replaced with peace to avoid self-inflicted pain by acknowledge the mistakes we have made, learnt some useful lesson, and use it a steppingstone to our next level.

Unless you let go of your past failures, by taking responsibility and acknowledge the truth of your past mistakes and errors, and the valuable lesson learnt from this bad experience, there is no chance of a new beginning and you cannot move forward properly. Failure or past mistakes are not what hinders us because everybody must have had some partial failure or mistakes at a certain point in life. The issue is our mindset, because challenges and failures are common factor to all human beings but what makes the difference is the ability to use them as valuable lessons and stepping-stones for success. That is, your challenges become your testimony, that is transformed to a subject of gratitude. We can thank God, for that challenge because it changed the course of our lives for good. The almighty God can convert your mistake to a miracle of success if you will co-operate with His plan and purpose for your life.

Do not allow past failure to hunt you, because it is quite easy to feel you would repeat your mistakes and failure. Look back for motivation and not for condemnation. Always have something to celebrate, no matter the value or size of the achievement. Be grateful to have attempted with courage any task. Keep reminding yourself with joy and be proud of what you have achieved or the courage and honour to attempt a failed difficult task. That should be used to encourage yourself and do not allow your past shortcomings and failures, to determine your future. We all make mistakes, so do not focus on the wrong things but be fully committed to achieve your next goal. However, we must be humble and be truthful (no self-denial or dishonesty) with ourselves, because that is the past-way to move forward to better things and a better life.

## Learn From Past Experiences

We all make mistakes and simply because we have lost our way does not mean that we are lost forever. In the end, what defines us is not our partial or past failures but the way we respond.

In the journey of life, the most essential thing is not that we make mistakes because we all do, but what really matters are our follow-up choices and decisions. This is what determines if we achieve our goals in life.

The secret is taken responsibility for our actions, make the necessary change in our attitude, be fully commitment and purposed to become successful.

## Learn To Deal with Failures

"Learn to do right; …" says Isaiah in chapter 1 verse 17 (NIV). There is no absolute perfect human being, so failure in something or certain area is always a possibility. However, this should not affect who we are, what we are and what we are capable of doing. Always remember that it is not that your partial or past failures that hinder you or prevent you from achieving your goals. A partial set back is only a delay and not a denial. There is no condition that is ever permanent, but temporary. Partial failures or mistakes should be acknowledged and used as a steppingstone to greater success. It is not partial failures that defeats us but our denial or refusal to acknowledge the mistake, learn from it and change.

We all make mistakes, have some kind of unsuccessful stories, and maybe disappointments. These happens to everyone but what makes the difference is our viewpoint, the way we see ourselves in light of difficulties, i.e., our mind-set. Do see it as inability to succeed, or do we see it as a stepping-stone to strive achieve our objectives? Do we see it as ways that we improve and can be better? Where is our focus? On the difficulties, partial failure, or search for solutions to overcome the obstacles? When our focus is wrong, our priorities will be bad, there is no room for change, unless we realize it and accept changes we may continue to fail. However, if we have the right priorities, acknowledge area where that needs improvement and bed courageous to make the necessary changes, we grow and succeed.

No matter how bad mistakes are in life, it is also a good school for those who are willing to learn from it and grow. It is a good thing to learn from the mistakes of other people, but the greatest lessons, although nobody likes it, are lessons from personal past mistakes. However, it terrible and awful refusing to admit mistakes, learn from past mistakes and partial failure because it hinders growth. Isaiah 1:17 (AKJV) says learn to do right or well, that means if we desire, we can learn from past failures to do well. Giving excuses or trying to be defensive by self-justification and not admitting them will prevent learning make impossible the changes we need to do well and grow. Finally, you only fail when you stop trying. That starts in your mind.

## Do not Let Other People's Negative Criticism Define You

In life everyone will encounter constructive and destructive words from different people like family members, friends, and others. i.e., evaluation from those we know and those we do not know. Criticism affects our values because it refers to good and negative judgment that is based on specific standards. Whatever the nature of the comments does not allow other people's negative attitude or criticism define your life. Why would anybody worry about other people's opinion they do not have control or cannot do anything about. Some people spend a lot of time worried or angry about what people think or say about them. It is sad wasting your precious time on things you cannot change. People lose their joy and peace because they are extremely sensitive and take every negative feedback too seriously.

Some people tend to feel personally offended when they receive criticism. Peace and joy are lost when we are overly sensitive and personally take every criticism. The reason we over-react is because we perceive it as an attack on us and our mind and thought tend to dwell continuously on it. Constructive and destructive criticism can be handled successfully by learning to establish its intent and practice responding calmly. We can also train ourselves not to re-act negatively and treat the person with love but without given him [or her] the opportunity to hurt us, but if they continue, we can actually cut ties with such negative person.

It is particularly important that whatever the situation we keep our peace with people and avoid angry reaction to their comments or any attempt to injure your self-esteem. Our self-worth or value does not depend on what people say or think about us but what the word of God sat about us. We must avoid allowing comment to make us lose sight of who we truly are and the unique qualities we have built within yourself. Therefore, soberly love yourself and anytime you receive destructive evaluation, speak to yourself positively. Our pep-talk or positive self-talk is more power than whatever anybody think or say about us. We should practice focusing on the useful suggestions. Our word should be, the criticism may be painful or even destructive, but it does not define me because I know who I am, in Christ Jesus. I am work in progress. I am confident of this, that he who began a good work in me will carry it on to completion until the day of Christ Jesus.

While some criticisms are destructive, some people may have valuable suggestions we need to take seriously into consideration for our growth. These evaluations should be used to humble us and become better person. We must take a personal valuable evaluation of our personal achievement by acknowledging the good things we have done and come to be on own talents, not hindered by other people's considerations. Our success in life will also depend on our ability and strength to take criticism and us it to our advantage to improve in various ways. We should appreciate constructive criticism because these people are interested in our success. Although we may feel sad or disappointed about the error or mistakes, their motives are good, and we should be grateful. Proverbs chapter 27 verse 5 to 6 (NIV), "Better is open rebuke than hidden love. Wounds from a friend can be trusted, but an enemy multiplies kisses."

We must take seriously control over our lives to avoid upsetting or overwhelming situations. We have freedom that comes from within by not taking negative criticism personally. We take control over our thoughts and do not allow our mind to wonder around the offence and judgments. We create boundaries that prevent anybody who held no significance in our lives to take from us "who we are" and put obstacles in the plan and purpose of God for our lives. There will always be someone who will make comments that does not reflect who we truly are, but we have the authority not to concede to them any power and most especially we do not allow them to define us. Believe in your-self and nobody can destroy your self-worth.

## Find a balance in your Life.

There is no common best life balance plan for mankind. Everyone has their own kind of balance in life plan based on their purposes and priorities. We all have different lives but living with real passion, set goals, routines and healthy relationship makes it easier to keep in balance. The good news is that we all make various choices and take decision about how to live our lives. Some of the decisions are personal while some involve other people. We make decision about activities and relationship based on our desire. There is balance in your life when you know your purposes and priorities and you diligently prioritize your activities.

The scripture in Mathew chapter 6 verse 33 (NIV), says "But seek first his kingdom and his righteousness, and all these things will be given to you as well." It is essential to know what matters in Life. This is actually the first step to living a balance life. The most essential thing is to seek God's kingdom and righteousness. Romans chapter 14 verse 17 through 19 (NIV), says "For the kingdom of God is not a matter of eating and drinking, but of righteousness, peace and joy in the Holy Spirit, because anyone who serves Christ in this way is pleasing to God and receives human approval. Let us therefore make every effort to do what leads to peace and to mutual edification."

A biblical perspective of the kingdom of God can be seen as Almighty God's universal reign as Creator and Christ's exhaustive work as our Redeemer. The kingdom of God is eternal, just as God is eternal. Therefore, God's Kingdom transcends time and space. When we submit our lives to the Lordship of Jesus Christ, and when He is in control of our lives, that is the kingdom of God. That is not having a lot of rules and regulations [do and not do lists], but "For the kingdom of God is not a matter of eating and drinking, but of righteousness, peace and joy in the Holy Spirit," Romans chapter 14 verse 17 (NIV), Yes, that is right standing with God, peace, and joy in life, that is awesome.

A balance life is a fruitful life, and this should be our focus as a Christian. Our Lord Jesus said, "For indeed, the kingdom of God is within you" Luke chapter 17 verse 21 (KJV). Let the rule of Jesus Christ on earth govern your life and take advantage of living the blessing and advantages that flow from His throne in Heaven. Psalm chapter 24 verse 1 (NIV), "The earth is the LORD's, and everything in it, the world, and all who live in it."

Romans chapter 1 verse 17, Hebrew chapter 10 verse 38, Habakkuk chapter 2 verse 4, and Galatians chapter 3 verse 11 all confirmed, "The Just shall live by Faith." Faith based in the wisdom and power of God is powerful and is the partway of a balance life. The plan and purpose of mankind directed by the wisdom of God in faith, love, integrity, and peace. When we live and act with kindness, joy, and integrity, we become confident about our actions and words.

We must have the right mind-set, a renewed mind based on the principles in the scriptures. Philippians chapter 2 verse 5 (NIV), says "In your relationships with one another, have the same mindset as Christ Jesus:" The best and most intelligent choice thing to maintain a balance in your life, is to acknowledge the need of a renewed mind. Whatsoever things are true, whatsoever things are honest, whatsoever things are just, whatsoever things are pure, whatsoever things are lovely, whatsoever things are of good report; if there be any virtue, and if there be any praise, think on these things. Romans chapter 12 verse 2 (NIV), says "Do not conform to the pattern of this world, but be transformed by the renewing of your mind. Then you will be able to test and approve what God's will is - his good, pleasing and perfect will."

Anyone can conquer fear because freedom is a state of the mind. The scripture in John chapter 8 verse 36 (NIV), says "So if the Son sets you free, you will be free indeed." Freedom and liberty in life is not doing everything you want or saying whatever you like but having a sound mind. It is not feeling guilty for the wrong choices or decisions of the past but making use of lesson learnt for growth. Balance is bringing things into harmony. It is something that you do continuously, rather than something that you can get.

However, there is peace and calmness when you realize that no matter how much you plan, things may not always go your way, i.e., you are human and not perfect [subject to errors and mistakes]. Be courageous and approach life as a whole avoiding distraction and dis-organization and certainly you do not organize your activities into separate disintegrated compartments. Stay focus always aware that you can integrate everything you do in your goal and plan,

Furthermore, you have other people to deal with, so unexpected events could always show up uninvited. A contingency plan or be open to re-schedule with rest and calmness. Run your schedule and do not let our schedule run our lives. So, take charge and govern your schedule and priorities. Be patient and perceive because your success is matter of time.

If your life takes a curve and you lose direction, control or for certain reasons you feel you are going through life without a clear purpose, you can always go back to the original plan where you have stated your highest values and priorities. Always acknowledge and accept your limitations and that you cannot do everything all the time. It is your responsibility to manage yourself properly. The ability to use wisely the power of choice and knowing what you do and having control over your life will bring balance.

## Rejection and Denial is Common

1 Peter chapter 2 verse 4 (NIV), says "As you come to him, the living Stone - rejected by humans but chosen by God and precious to him -." Our Lord Jesus Christ is the living stone that was rejected by mankind but chosen and precious in God's sight. Rejection is the act of refusing to accept, use or believe someone or something. In the journey of life, we all have to deal with rejection. This could also be the act of not giving someone the love and attention they want and expect. Rejection is a part of life. It could happen to anyone at any stage in life. There is no escape, at some point in life every person has to deals with some form of rejection.

Maybe, you have been rejected, or maybe you have rejected someone in the past. The hard truth is that rejection is something none of us can really avoid. There is no anti-dot or something that prevents or counteracts rejection from happing, because it does happen to everybody. It could come from members of the family, relatives, romantic relations, and friendship. There are various types and magnitude of rejections. Some larger forms are more difficult to cope with than the lighter forms of common rejections. No matter what form or manner the results are deep emotions hurts and could be very painful.

Whatever is the state, rejection is unpleasant and exceedingly difficult to accept. It is a very painful experience, and the effects sometimes lingers for a long time. If not addressed properly this painful experience can remain with the person for an awfully long time. The scriptures remind us that nobody is exempted, it could happen to everyone. Our Lord Jesus was rejected by his own people. Apostle Peter denied Jesus three times, when Jesus was taken to be crucified. In John chapter 1 verse 11 (ESV), tells us that He came to his own, and his own people did not receive him. The book of Isaiah chapter 53 verse 3 (NIV), gives us this powerful picture of rejection, "He was despised and rejected by mankind, a man of suffering, and familiar with pain. Like one from whom people hide their faces he was despised, and we held him in low esteem.!"

We have hope because our High Priest was also rejected. These are feelings of sadness, shame, and even grief. Some people are filled with sorrow and terrible suffering, when they are not accepted by others, like the end of a relationship, a feeling of not being accepted within the family or friendship. This act of being rejected creates negative feelings and emotions that are difficult to overcome because they attack the soul and steal the peace of the person. This could also result in fear, loneliness, and isolation and in worst cases depression.

The good news is that we can come out of the valley of rejection, better than what we were before we got into it. The scripture reminds us, that Jesus our High Priest will never leave us nor forsake us, but will always be there for us, to ease the bitterness of rejection. Hebrews chapter 4 verse 15 (NIV), says "For we do not have a high priest who is unable to empathize with our weaknesses, but we have one who has been tempted in every way, just as we are - yet he did not sin." That is why Jesus suffered for us. There is no cause for shame because we know whom we have believed, and we are convinced that He is able to guard what we have entrusted to Him until that day. So, there is hope because God's grace is sufficient for us in our weakness, to bring us to the other side. Job chapter 19 verse 25 (NIV), says this, "I know that my redeemer lives, and that in the end he will stand on the earth." If we allow Him, God heals the heart, from pain to peace.

## Accept and let it Go!

Patient is the steppingstone to peace. Personal success as the highest aspiration anyone wants to achieve. Most people want to achieve great hights but afraid of any failure that damaged their confident. Some have lost one of the greatest paths to success "self-motivation". They have no zeal to motivate themselves because they feel better about their present condition listening and depending on others to show them everything they should do or must not do in life. There is nothing against motivator, let us be clear about that, but motivators need to encourage individual to stir-up the talents which are in them through the grace of God. Apostle Paul told Timothy in the book 2 Timothy chapter 1 verses 6 through 7 (NIV), says "For this reason I remind you to fan into flame the gift of God, which is in you through the laying on of my hands. For the Spirit God gave us does not make us timid, but gives us power, love and self-discipline."

We must encourage everyone to pursue their dreams and instruct them that every goal in life is achievable by commitment and striving, but also remind them that failure is possible. There are moments in life that you are holding on to the thing because something you are holding onto may not be worth keeping. That is the time to let it go. There are times when it more profitable to be patient and instead of taking on the excess baggage that significantly slows you down in your journey. There is a time or season, to have a self-critical proper look at your goals to assess correctly what is absolutely necessary and what should let go.

All things will not always go as planned. When the plan involves other people, a time may come when their chapter in the journey should close, a time to let go and move forward to the other side with fresh ideas and different people. There are times no matter how hard you try or how much effort or time you put in; it may not always guarantee that the goals will always be achieved. Reschedule is not a failure, it a part of the plan. There are times and season in life that we face major obstacles internal or external and no matter how hard or much time you try the obstacles is intact i.e., remain unsurmountable.

A change or modification of the original plan is not a failure, it is necessary to determine the areas to invest profitably our time and efforts to successfully achieve our desire and goals. My Friends, nobody has absolute control what other people does or does not do, there are some situations beyond our ability and control. In the event of these challenges, trials, and crisis, i.e., situation or circumstance that we cannot change the best option is to let go.!

## Ask and Wait for the Season

The 1 John 5 chapter 14 through 16 (NIV), tells us "This is the confidence we have in approaching God: that if we ask anything according to his will, he hears us. And if we know that he hears us - whatever we ask - we know that we have what we asked of him." When praying about a situation in our family and discover that waiting is needed for a breakthrough, it could become a challenge if not properly confronted with patient, thanksgiving, and praises. The challenge we face is that during waiting period there is a feeling that seems there no progress, but a standstill in our situation. Waiting is not struggling, worrying, and stressing but an intentional choice to trust God, and patiently expect something that we do not have complete control. The word wait is "to serve", [or "to look for"] which means to expect something. Hopefully, a confident expectation for something good, and it all depends on our attitude and mind-set.

The attitude should be our hearts are steadfast, trusting in the Lord, because our waiting is a waiting on [or waiting for] God's goodness and lovingkindness. A positive anticipation, and expectation for God's goodness and blessing. A joyful confident hope in something we are believing for that will take place soon. It is a vital part of life [life is full of waiting], i.e. when we pray, there is a period to wait for an answer to our request. The truth is, "wait," can be listed among the most challenging exhortations in the Bible. This ability to wait on the Lord comes from our trust, a confident expectation, as we focused on who God's is, His principles, Word, promises, and what God has done and is doing. We know and have trust in the plan, purpose, and power of the almighty God.

The scripture says that our children will be mighty in the land; the generation of the upright will be blessed. Wealth and riches are in their houses. The word of God is the wisdom of God, and it says God is love. The scriptures show us that Job in his challenges prayed for his friends, we should likewise learn to focus on encouraging and assisting people who are in need through prayer and kind words. This essential decision will move our attention from ourselves and gives us a better perspective on our own struggles and challenges in life. That is to continue seeking the godly counsel and wisdom about the situation. This gives us knowledge and understanding to have confident in the love, wisdom, and timing of God.

We agree with the Word in Psalm 27, I am still confident of this: I will see the goodness of the Lord in the land of the living. Wait for the Lord; be strong and take heart and wait for the Lord. To wait has great benefits notwithstanding the fact some of us may not like the idea of waiting and could become impatience in the process. Having fellowship with the Holy Spirit bring us into the treasure of God's provision and timing for our situation. The danger of loss of fellowship with the Lord is impatience, lack of and spiritual wisdom and strength.

## Fear Not

The scripture says in Isaiah chapter 26 verses 3 to 4 (NIV), "You will keep in perfect peace those whose minds are steadfast, because they trust in you. Trust in the LORD forever, for the LORD, the LORD himself, is the Rock eternal.". Fear is a human emotion designed to help us, by alerting us to danger so that we will act against it. As written in Psalm chapter 56 verse 3 (NIV), "When I am afraid, I put my trust in you." Fear starts with a lie, but if we allow it to take deep root in us and control us, so that we live in constant worry, despair, and panic it becomes demonic. Fear is a thief, that actually steal our joy and peace. To live continually in fear is self-disrespecting and self-punishment.

There are times when we have difficulties reconciling the goodness of God with challenging and difficult circumstances. This produces doubt, worry, anxiety and it takes a toll on our trust in the promises of God. We must be crystal clear on our priorities and focus on God through the written word, to avoid frustration distrust and fear. God does not want us to live in doubt, hopeless, and disoriented but to trust in His faithfulness and everlasting love for us. In Isaiah chapter 41 verse 10 (NIV), God reassures us, "So do not fear, for I am with you; do not be dismayed, for I am your God. I will strengthen you and help you; I will uphold you with my righteous right hand."

Our attitude should always be in God, whose word I praise, in God I trust; I will not be afraid. This is what God expects from us, to trust and be confident of His love for us, rather than given way to fear. We must learn from the scriptures to walk by faith and not sight, i.e., to walk from fear to faith. God know about all about our individual needs and essentials for daily life, so we want us to be free from worry and anxiety. 1 John chapter 4 verse 18 (NIV), says "There is no fear in love. But perfect love drives out fear because fear has to do with punishment. The one who fears is not made perfect in love."

John chapter 14 verse 27 (NIV), "Peace I leave with you; my peace I give you. I do not give to you as the world gives. Do not let your hearts be troubled and do not be afraid." God is everywhere and certainly knowing everything about you, what is going on in your life, all your desires and how best to meet those desires. He loves to satisfy the desire of your heart. So, we must identify source of these lies are from the forces of darkness and replace them by the truth in the word and position ourselves to be a receiver of God's goodness. This is how we position ourselves to overcome fear.

2 Timothy chapter 1 verse 9 (NIV), says, "He has saved us and called us to a holy life - not because of anything we have done but because of his own purpose and grace. This grace was given us in Christ Jesus before the beginning of time." There are various types of fear the forces of darkness use as strategies to steal your confidence, joy, faith, and peace. Fear of the future, loneliness, joblessness, finance, rejection, diseases, sickness, conflict, war, past secrets, intimacy, heights, accident, death etc…... Fear that what God promises will never come to pass. Be still and know that God is God but if you focus your thoughts and mind on your situation or continue to have false imagination of forth coming circumstances or events, fear will a grip your life. The problem is your thoughts and wrongly believe that you have to confront the situation alone, in our own strength. Philippians chapter 4 verses 6 to 7 (NIV), reminds us "Do not be anxious about anything, but in every situation, by prayer and petition, with thanksgiving, present your requests to God. And the peace of God, which transcends all understanding, will guard your hearts and your minds in Christ Jesus." The goal of the enemy of your soul is to drains your emotional and physical strength. This could eventually weaken your faith and living a Christian.

However, there is good news because in the Scriptures, we are repeatedly reminded by God's response to fear, "Do not fear!" or "Don't be afraid!" We must fight the fight of faith by "fighting fear" always remembering ourselves that we are the children of God's love. God promises us "I am with you." We must believe, trust, and have faith in God. The just shall live by faith - Habakkuk 2:4, Romans 1:17, Galatians 3:11, and Hebrews 10:38

Habakkuk chapter 2 verse 4 (NIV), "See, the enemy is puffed up; his desires are not upright - but the righteous person will live by his faithfulness -"

Romans chapter 1 verse 17 (NIV), "For in the gospel the righteousness of God is revealed - a righteousness that is by faith from first to last, just as it is written: The righteous will live by faith."

Galatians chapter 3 verse 11 (NIV), "Clearly no one who relies on the law is justified before God, because the righteous will live by faith."

Hebrews 10:38 (NIV), "But my righteous[a] one will live by faith. And I take no pleasure in the one who shrinks back."

Psalm chapter 94 verse 19 (NIV), says "When anxiety was great within me, your consolation brought me joy." God is our source. In the event of painful rejection, the Holy Spirit will assist us to modify any problematic behaviour, by correcting the offending behaviour, to prevent future rejection, giving us the power to live a joyful and peaceful life. We can always trust and depend on God's unconditional love, integrity, and faithfulness to strengthen and protect us. We belong to God, and His power saves, helps, empowers, and provides for all our needs according to His riches in glory. The almighty will never leave us or forsake us but will walk with us through any and every crisis, assisting us to handle the challenges peacefully according to His grace.

## Cultivate Good Habits or Routines

To enjoy the journey of life and have peace we must learn the power to focus on few good habits at a time. Set goals, learn, be committed, focused, and motivated to live your best life. Your plan should inspire you to succeed. We all regardless of age, race, or belief, through repeated actions has developed some familiar routines consciously or unconsciously, in our daily lifestyle. These routines known as habits may beneficial or harmful to our lives. The habits we desire and suggested in previous pages of this book are beneficiary and must be chosen on purpose to make us successful in life.

## Be strong in the Lord and in the power of His Might!

Ephesians chapter 6 verse 10 (NIV), says "Finally, be strong in the Lord and in his mighty power." The word "be strong" refers to "be strengthened, in the Lord and in the strength of His power." We are reminded and encouraged to trust and remain faithfulness to our calling in the power of the almighty God. Our faith for everything we need in life should be anchored in the power that supplies our needs according to His riches in glory. God is our source, and He empowers us to be proper. Our dependence on God is not a weakness, because when we are weak, we are strong in the power of His might. We are able to do all things through him who strengthens us.

Jesus says in John chapter 15 verses 5 to 7 (NIV), "I am the vine; you are the branches. If you remain in me and I in you, you will bear much fruit; apart from me you can do nothing. If you do not remain in me, you are like a branch that is thrown away and withers; such branches are picked up, thrown into the fire, and burned. If you remain in me and my words remain in you, ask whatever you wish, and it will be done for you." This is to my father's glory, that you bear much fruit, showing yourselves to be my disciples. The Lord Jesus Christ gives power to the believer to be fruitful in life. If you remain in Him and He in you, you will bear much fruit; apart from Him you can do nothing. The scripture says, we as believers in Christ we have at our disposal all the strength of His might. We have gifts and talents given to us and the ability to be able to succeed in life. This also indicates that we have available to us what it takes to meet His plan and purpose for our life. If we are committed to walk diligently with God, we will receive all the strength to accomplish with success everything we have do in our daily, monthly, and yearly tasks. We are strong "in the Lord," and in the power His might. We are victorious and can do all things through Christ, who empowers me. In the event of challenges, setbacks, and difficulties we have peace because we trust God and always keep on expecting ultimate victory on the other side.

Life becomes joyful and peaceful when we realize, believe, and have faith about what God can and will do on our behalf that trust Him. This gives us focus and makes us strong in the Lord to confront the challenges of life. 1 Corinthians chapter 2 verse 9 to 10 (NIV), says "However, as it is written: "What no eye has seen, what no ear has heard, and what no human mind has conceived - the things God has prepared for those who love him - these are the things God has revealed to us by his Spirit. The Spirit searches all things, even the deep things of God." We trust God and keep expecting victory even when we are confronted by setbacks, trials, challenges, and difficulties. The wisdom and knowledge of what God can and will do on our behalf is part of what makes us strong in the Lord and in the power of His might.

## Rejoice Always

Ecclesiastes chapter 5 verses 19 to 20 (NIV), "Moreover, when God gives someone wealth and possessions, and the ability to enjoy them, to accept their lot and be happy in their toil - this is a gift of God. They seldom reflect on the days of their life, because God keeps them occupied with gladness of heart."

Nehemiah chapter 8 verse 10 (NIV), "....... for the joy of the LORD is your strength." The joy of the Lord is what gives us the strength not to give up, to be courageous and to keep steady in the event of difficult and hard circumstances. The Joy of the Lord gives peace and the ability to stay in faith, with praises and thanksgiving, instead of worry and complaining. Joy gives us stability and the power of champions, never to give up or abandon our plan. Proverbs chapter 16 verse 3 (NIV), "Commit to the LORD whatever you do, and he will establish your plans." Our rugged determination should always be an extraordinarily strong commitment to always trust and obey God as the only way to be happy, peaceful, and successful in life. Be discipline as a disciple of Jesus Christ, walk by faith, hoping for the best, trusting God, love God and whatever you do, do it with excellent spirit as unto the Lord rejoicing always.

"Dear friend, I pray that you may enjoy good health and that all may go well with you, even as your soul is getting along well. It gave me great joy when some believers came and testified about your faithfulness to the truth, telling how you continue to walk in it. I have no greater joy than to hear that my children are walking in the truth." -3 John chapter 1 verses 2 to 4 (NIV).

"Rejoice in the Lord always. I will say it again: Rejoice!" - Philippians chapter 4 verse 4 (NIV).

"Rejoice always." - 1 Thessalonians chapter 5 verse 16 (NIV).

"Finally, my brethren, rejoice in the Lord. For me to write the same things to you *is* not tedious, but for you *it is* safe." - Philippians chapter 3 verse 1 (NKJV).

Printed in the United States
by Baker & Taylor Publisher Services